OUT OF THE ORDINARY

Alex Vickery-Howe

CURRENT THEATRE SERIES

First published in 2016
by Currency Press Pty Ltd,
PO Box 2287, Strawberry Hills, NSW, 2012, Australia
enquiries@currency.com.au
www.currency.com.au

in association with Accidental Productions

Copyright: *Out of the Ordinary* © Alex Vickery-Howe, 2016.

COPYING FOR EDUCATIONAL PURPOSES
The Australian *Copyright Act 1968* (Act) allows a maximum of one chapter or 10% of this book, whichever is the greater, to be copied by any educational institution for its educational purposes provided that that educational institution (or the body that administers it) has given a remuneration notice to Copyright Agency Limited (CAL) under the Act.
For details of the CAL licence for educational institutions contact CAL, 11/66 Goulburn Street, Sydney, NSW, 2000; tel: within Australia 1800 066 844 toll free; outside Australia 61 2 9394 7600; fax: 61 2 9394 7601; email: info@copyright.com.au

COPYING FOR OTHER PURPOSES
Except as permitted under the Act, for example a fair dealing for the purposes of study, research, criticism or review, no part of this book may be reproduced, stored in a retrieval system, or transmitted in any form or by any means without prior written permission. All enquiries should be made to the publisher at the address above.

Any performance or public reading of *Out of the Ordinary* is forbidden unless a licence has been received from the author or the author's agent. The purchase of this book in no way gives the purchaser the right to perform the play in public, whether by means of a staged production or a reading. All applications for public performance should be addressed to the author C/- Currency Press.

Cataloguing-in-publication data for this title is available from the National Library of Australia website: www.nla.gov.au

Typeset by Dean Nottle for Currency Press.
Cover and internal artwork by Nick Rees.

Currency Press acknowledges the Traditional Owners of the Country on which we live and work. We pay our respects to all Aboriginal and Torres Strait Islander Elders, past and present.

Contents

Introduction: The Art of Life
by Dr Maggie Ivanova   v

OUT OF THE ORDINARY

   Act One: Bad Week   1

   Act Two: Glorious   49

Theatre Program at the end of the playtext

INTRODUCTION: THE ART OF LIFE

AESTHETIC ENGAGEMENTS WITH THE EVERYDAY

Jean-Jacques Rousseau, the Romantic philosopher, begins Book I of his *Confessions* (1782) with a claim to self-understanding and uniqueness which is without precedent in Western culture: 'I know my heart, and have studied mankind; I am not made like any one I have been acquainted with, perhaps like no one in existence', he assures his audience, and offers a rather striking conclusion: 'if not better, I at least claim originality'. Rousseau is fully aware that he is giving an interpretative, performative expression to his life experiences and intimate feelings. His *Confessions* are, after all, his autobiography, an act of self-generation. And it is hardly accidental that he offered public readings of sections of the manuscript before its first part appeared in print posthumously: 'I have entered upon a performance which is without example, whose accomplishment will have no imitator. I mean to present my fellow-mortals with a man in all the integrity of nature; and this man shall be myself.'

Confident that 'Nature did wisely in breaking the mould with which she formed [him]', and expecting little if any disagreement from us, Rousseau stands tall as a co-creator. In his autobiography, he presents a fulfilling, though at times historically unfaithful, reenactment of his inner and outer world in which we can recognise not only the creative cult to feeling but also a cult to the self. His is a creativity grounded in the pleasures of the imagination whose expressive powers are now transformed into lived experiences. Western culture is just a step away from embracing a vision of human life as an ongoing 'project' of self-fashioning and self-expression. And the less ordinary the quest and experience, the better. Next, we learn how to package, market and sell the desire for uniqueness and expectations of extraordinary lived experiences, making them ready for consumption.

Enter Jasper Sprout. Jasper is in desperate need of renewal; he yearns to relive his career as a rock musician, which prematurely ended with the birth of his daughter, aptly named Theodora (in Greek, 'God's gift'). Dramatic irony? Likely. One wonders also if it is really profound self-realisation that Jasper seeks. Perhaps the 'primal self' or the 'dream' he is after is a reflection of an impulse in contemporary culture to amplify our experiences, no matter how mundane, in order to heighten their emotional intensity and make them worthy of dramatic replay—whether through personal reminiscences, tweets or Facebook posts (accompanied by selfies, of course) intended for family or friends or, better yet, total strangers. Jasper reenacts such a dramatic replay through his collection of newspaper reviews of his 'enviable vocal range'. He wants to be envied and admired again; he wants to be compared favorably to legends like young Elvis or Eddie Vedder.

Or is it an existential crisis that Jasper is going through? This is certainly a possibility. Perhaps on some level he is indeed struggling to accept that his daughter's birth marked the beginning of the end of his (creative) life: 'You used to look up to me then. I could see it in your eyes. What happened to your eyes, Theo?' And what are the implications of his total lack of awareness of his little girl's pregnancy? Theo is actually in her twenties, and this is precisely the point. Perhaps Jasper's 'blindness' or, alternatively, the 'selective vision' of his complete self-absorption are the instruments of self-deception, a self-defense mechanism: after all, he is 'too sexy to be a granddad', definitely not ready to lose to a granddaughter in the smooth skin competition. This is hardly the life purpose he has imagined for himself. Whatever the motivation for Jasper's soul-searching, however, it is never too late to meet his true self.

Enter Chad Mombardo, the self-made guru in the business of fashioning and selling dreams, with just the right package for Jasper. He also knows how to promote it: 'To find your true self, you need more than a mirror. You need open eyes, open heart and open soul.' His words reach Jasper though a cassette tape … for greater authenticity! However, it would be rather disingenuous, and even cynical, to assume that what Chad calls openness is equivalent only to an open purse, with a large line of credit, a pinch of imagination and a lot of self-love. Like a Dostoevskian anti-hero, Chad might be increasingly harder to like as the play progresses but we simply cannot dismiss what he has to say: obsessed with novelty and afraid of the ordinary, we chase the extraordinary even if we have to manufacture it ourselves and even when we fail to capture it in the end. Most of us will fail because the

Susan Boyles in this world are rare talents, indeed! How many of us can wipe off the condescending smiles of Simon Cowell, Amanda Holden and Piers Morgan, and with just a few notes of divine singing transform their full-of-ridicule rolling eyes into pure amazement, to a house roaring with applause? It is hardly accidental that 'extraordinary' is the word each of the judges of *Britain's Got Talent 3* (2009) used to describe their experience. This is Jasper's dream.

To an extent, this is also the dream of Wallace and his friends, Figsby and Sasha. They, too, see themselves as different and special. Their sense of 'being extraordinary' lies in a search for social transformation which they believe they should undertake on their own because those currently in power are driven by routine. The fact that their political formation has only seven supporters, or perhaps three and a half, is a minor dent in their plan. What matters is the top name on the ticket ... and also that someone brings chips and punch to enhance the experience. 'We'll cling to anyone who dangles a carrot,' Chad warns us, to anyone who tells us that our potential is limitless and promises to make it even bigger. Or, as anthropologist Roger D. Abrahams explains:

> Because our individual experiences are so central to the ways in which we put together a sense of our own identity, to underscore the typicality [*read 'ordinariness'*] is to confront one of our dearest held beliefs: that having been made individuals, we should do everything we can to hold on to our sense of uniqueness. Yet experience tells us that what happens to us is never so original ... especially as we recognize ourselves as members of a generation, a network, a community. (1986: 50, my addition and emphasis.)

The danger (or entrepreneurial opportunity) to which Chad refers in Act II of the play—while the elemental storm strengthens and threatens to engulf Theo and Anni—comes from such an unwillingness to confront this dearest of all beliefs. Our holding on to it feeds consumer culture and its ideology. As sociologists and market researchers point out, among the strongest forces driving consumer culture are the elements of 'failure' and 'disappointment', coupled with the persuasive rhetoric that we control our destinies and can fashion ourselves accordingly through consumption: this explains why we 'are consumed with consumption, take pleasure from pleasure, desire to desire and want to want'. (Brown et al. 1998: 8)

Theo, however, is different. All she wants from life is to be normal, to be surrounded by 'ordinary people doing their best. Just hanging out together, touching each other's lives, spinning around the sun …' She does not need to stand in the spotlight or create legendary legacy; she makes no promises to anyone about an extraordinary life, certainly not to Wallace or their yet-to-be-born baby girl Anni (short for Anesidora, Greek for 'giver of gifts'). An intriguing inversion in generational characterisation is at play here: contrary to our expectations, it is Jasper and Babs who are the restless spirits feeding on extraordinary experiences. Theirs is a home of bright colours and remarkable spiritual objects, acquired through an alternative lifestyle and travels to Asia and South America in search of a 'primal self'. Both in their forties, Jasper and Babs behave like Theo's hip young friends (though they are the only ones buying their image). It is Theo's task to bring them down to earth, to create harmony. In a humorous way, the Sprouts' is a home ruled by filiarchy—it is the daughter who calls the tune (from *filia*, Latin for 'daughter'). Perhaps this is what makes her their divine gift. Anesidora, however, is both Theodora's double and her gadfly (in its Socratic meaning). Anni's name bears associations with two earth goddesses—Demeter (harvest, agriculture, fertility) and Gaia (primordial Mother Earth). If Theo is what Babs and Jasper need most, Anni fulfills the same function for Theo. Through evocative association in Greek mythology with Pandora, Anesidora's appearance one morning opens up the box of Theo's greatest fears and insecurities. It is this experience that allows us to see the extraordinary in the very ordinary, the different in the normal, the beautiful in the everyday, the art in maths and, last but not least, the aesthetics of gingham.

The Janus-faced relationship between Theo and Anni is hyper-real, rather than merely imaginative. Anni does exist. This is why she is physicalised on stage by a separate actor. Perhaps she and Theo make two, opposing at first and then mutually complementary, parts of Theo's personality, a hyper-reality created through the realisation of pregnancy. Whatever line of interpretation we take, it is necessary to appreciate that such an approach to characterisation through the hyper-real is commonly found in popular culture, especially in North American comics and Japanese manga and anime. The experience of the hyper-real results from a hybrid, multimodal meaning-making relationship between the verbal, the visual and the ambiguous (spiritual, irrational or plain bizarre and inexplicable). A world similar to those we see in comics and manga, which are dramaturgically evoked here, creates a primary reality that serves as a meeting point for separate expressive and experiential planes—Theo and Anni, thought and emotion, word and image, here and elsewhere.

These resemble the various planes of experience, or alternative realities, which often intersect in the fictional worlds of Japanese novelist and short story writer Haruki Murakami. The psychic connections and physical interactions between Anni and Theo, for example, resonate with those between Crow and Kafka in *Kafka on the Shore* (2002); during the elemental storm in Act II, Theo's personal 'Pandora's box' acquires the tangible spatiality of the time-unspecific attic full of skeletons or the mysterious room of the Sheep Man on the sixteenth floor of the Dolphin Hotel in *Dance, Dance, Dance* (1988). Lewis Carroll fans, of course, also recognise this aesthetic phenomenon: Carroll's fiction offers multiple and varied examples of parallel worlds, and dreams that are not quite dreams. The image of the Cheshire Cat, distinctly whimsical in his unexpected appearances and disappearances, is perhaps the most powerful trigger or symptom of different, briefly intersecting planes of experience in Carroll's work.

So Theo decides to leave her Pandora's box open and faces her fiercest demons. Instead of trying to fit in with everyone around her who insists on being special, she chooses simply to be different and ordinary, to embrace the moment and to try to become a kind mother. Gingham continues to define her but, similar to her approach to maths, she lets her passion and creativity lead. Who needs the role models of Judy Garland in *The Wizard of Oz*, Katherine Hepburn in *The Philadelphia Story*, Marilyn Monroe and her tight gingham shirts, or Brigitte Bardot in her pink gingham wedding dress? And who says that one cannot have an aesthetic attitude towards non-art? Isn't it possible to engage aesthetically with wrapping or opening a package, with having a cup of tea, or with cooking? As philosopher Jerome Stolnitz pointed out astutely during the Pop Art era, an observer's attitude can transform anything into an object worthy of aesthetic attention, even if this 'object' is conceptual thought. The aesthetics of maths. The art of everyday life. This is why, instead of seeking the extraordinary in the world, Theo decides to focus on the here-and-now, and to introduce Anni to her family: 'We clash. We confuse each other. We say cruel things', she admits. 'But, nobody knows us the way we know us. In our tiny corner of the world, we are the stars of our own little soap opera. For me that's enough to build a life around.' In this sincere and affectionate attitude to her family, one cannot but help hearing creative echoes from *The Munsters* or *The Addams Family*: each family member's repeated attempts to fit in with the social mainstream, to be 'normal', only reaffirm his or her need to be different, to cherish the monster within. Compared to the idiosyncrasies and quirkiness in ordinary human beings, the demon of conformity is far more disturbing.

Dr Maggie Ivanova
Director of Studies, Drama, Flinders University
September 2016, Adelaide

Further reading:

Abrahams, R. D. 1986. 'Ordinary and Extraordinary Experience' in *The Anthropology of Experience*. Ed. by Victor W. Turner and Edward M. Bruner (Urbana and Chicago: University of Illinois Press). pp. 45-72.

Brown. S., A.M. Doherty and B. Clark (eds.). 1998. *Romancing the Market* (London: Routledge).

Rousseau, J.J. 1903. *The Confessions of Jean-Jacques Rousseau*. Privately Printed for the Members of the Aldus Society, London. Project Gutenberg E-book. Released 2015, last update 2016. Online.

Out of the Ordinary was first produced by Accidental Productions at the Bakehouse Theatre, Adelaide, on 4 October 2016, with the following cast:

ANESIDORA	Maya Aleksandra
THEODORA	Steph Clapp
JASPER / SECOND CRITIC / KING OF SWING	Brendan Cooney
WALLACE / FOURTH CRITIC / TOWN CRIER	Robbie Greenwell
CHAD / THIRD CRITIC / APOTHECARY	Alec S. Hall
SASHA / SIXTH CRITIC / LIAR BIRD	Mikayla Lynch
FIGSBY / FIFTH CRITIC / MAGIC FROG	Nomakhosi Mpala
BARBARA / FIRST CRITIC / QUEEN BARBARELLA	Josephine Pugh

Director, Joh Hartog
Set and Costume Designers, Kirsty Martinsen / Alison Stamke / Casey van Sebille
Sound and Lighting Designer, Stephen Dean
Stage Manager, Lauren Taylor
Mathematics Advisor, Dr Virginia Kinnear

CHARACTERS

THEODORA SPROUT (THEO), a hipster girl in her 20s, prematurely worn down by life. Two parts Daria, one part Olive Penderghast. Glasses. Gingham. Feisty attitude.

ANESIDORA SPROUT (ANNI), Theo's more vibrant, self-assured twin. Uninhibited. Fast-talking. Slightly mad.

BARBARA SPROUT (BABS), Theo's mother, early 40s. Sweet-natured, but quietly powerful. Conservative clothing. Excessive blush. Generous smile. Her comments are layered with subtext.

JASPER SPROUT, Theo's father, 40s. A washed-up ex-singer. He tries to put on a charming façade, but he's a little defeated inside. Feral beard. Rock regalia. Behind the times.

CHAD MOMBARDO, early 30s, a snake oil salesman oozing empty promises and superficial charisma. Venomous when provoked.

WALLACE, Theo's boyfriend. Self-consciously bohemian and goofy, but thoughtful and warm-hearted. Even when he's angry, he's adorable.

FIGSBY, Wallace's best friend. Equally passionate about revolutionary action and four-cheese pizza. Subversive. Confident. A shrewd observer of everyone around her.

SASHA, Wallace's campaign manager. Tough. Withering. Thin-skinned. Prone to bursts of euphoria as well as sudden condemnations, owing to her nicotine comedown.

STAGE HAND

CRITICS (six)

QUEEN BARBARELLA

KING OF SWING

APOTHECARY

TOWN CRIER

MAGIC FROG

LIAR BIRD

Suggested character pairings:

BARBARA SPROUT / FIRST CRITIC / QUEEN BARBARELLA

JASPER SPROUT / SECOND CRITIC / KING OF SWING

CHAD MOMBARDO / THIRD CRITIC / APOTHECARY

WALLACE / FOURTH CRITIC / TOWN CRIER

FIGSBY / FIFTH CRITIC / MAGIC FROG

SASHA / SIXTH CRITIC / LIAR BIRD

SETTING

An exciting 'rock world', where iconography related to music, pop culture and celebrity dominates the set. Seemingly normal encounters are interwoven with sudden fantasy sequences, musical numbers, cartoonish projections and exaggarated sound effects. The audience should feel like they're attending a concert, or perhaps they've dropped acid.

Despite Theo's assertions that her life should be 'ordinary', the *mise en scène* is kicking her ass at every turn. Nothing is constant in this world—locations bleed together, the impossible blends with the mundane and words are powerful.

Sequences involving Anni have an even stronger touch of 'unreality' about them. Whenever Theo and Anni get close it makes Theo physically uncomfortable, triggering nausea and tremors. There are hallucinatory qualities to these encounters, accentuated by changes in sound and vision, as though the world shifts to an odd angle whenever Anni appears.

As the antagonist, Chad has a negative effect on the environment. While he initially conceals his cruel nature with a playful façade, something inhuman lurks behind his pearly smile. He's more than a common swindler—his words are toxic. As these layers peel away, a storm threatens to tear Theo's world apart. Chad becomes an elemental force in Theo's life, a predator stalking her family home.

WRITER'S NOTE

This is a fast-paced play. A beat is a beat, not a pause, and the cast should be exhausted by the end. Theo, in particular, has to balance articulate delivery with high energy levels. Her mathematical calculations and direct audience addresses should be brisk, engaging and hyper.

Nobody ever gets truly angry in this play. Dialogue may appear pointed, or even cruel, but this is banter between family and friends who love each other deeply. They exchange barbs that bounce off as though their clothes were Teflon, and nobody pauses long enough to take deep offense. For these characters, communication is snappy and colourful. Only Theo's relationship with Jasper is in real jeopardy and that relates more to what is not said between them, until the end.

Above all else, this is a magical play. It flows with dream logic … because life is never ordinary.

Forward slashes (/) indicate interruptions; the point at which the next line of dialogue begins.

This play went to press before the end of rehearsals and may differ from the play as performed.

ACT ONE: BAD WEEK

SCENE ONE

Pink lighting. The stage is swimming in rock memorabilia—the tackier the better—from Elvis clocks to wall-mounted guitars, from gleaming Ziggy Stardust eyes to slobbering Mick Jagger tongues. A baby grand piano sits stage right, beneath a twirling mirror ball. Downstage left, a little stool lies tangled in purple knitting beside a modest dining table. An altar, complete with a hissing effigy, occupies the centre.

Behind, the back wall is smothered in images of famous artists of varied tastes, talents and styles: William Shakespeare, Boy George, Andy Warhol, Liza Minnelli, Vincent van Gogh, Sidney Poitier, Pink, Ludwig van Beethoven, Joni Mitchell, Alfred Hitchcock, Emily Brontë, Jim Henson, Truman Capote and Virginia Woolf, to name but a few possibilities. Anyone who has ever been anyone throughout history. 'High art' and pop culture overlap in a striking poster collage.

'Crocodile Rock' (Elton John) plays.

Gradually, the lights dim until the stage is just a faint pink blush. The music slows, taking on a slightly sad, slightly sinister feel. Finally, the record dies altogether and all we are left with is a needle scratch.

THEODORA SPROUT, *early twenties, enters the room, shakes her head at all the crap and takes a nervous look around to make sure she is alone. Satisfied, she rolls herself a joint.*

THEO: My father is … interesting. That's not a compliment.

    She takes a moment to lick the paper and let out a sigh.

Do you see this place? Are you *really* looking at my world? Those bulbs are pink. Pink!

    Beat.

    She lights up the joint, takes a drag and hunts for an ashtray.

I'm moving out in two months. A month and a half if I can afford it. [*Grinning*] I'm Theo, by the way.

An ashtray glitters from on top of the piano, catching her eye. THEO *scoops it up.*

All of this is Dad's idea of elegant. Check out the guitars, the tongues, the altar … yes, that's an altar … Dad is always auditioning a new icon. It's Nergal's turn this week. Nergal is the Mesopotamian god of destruction and war. [*She sighs.*] It's been a bad week.

She sits down on the stool, smoking thoughtfully.

Mum is more traditional. She knits, she scolds, she laments.

She takes a drag.

It sucks being an only child. There's nobody to share the load, or to take the flak when things get tense. Not that things are really all that tense around here. Not yet, at least. But the explosion is coming. I can feel myself lighting a fuse.

BABS: [*offstage*] Theodora, is that something illegal I smell?
THEO: Shit!

She pushes the joint into the ashtray.

BABS: [*offstage*] If you're smoking again, you'll have to go back to the reverend for a tune-up.

THEO *shudders.*

THEO: Eeew. [*Calling*] I'm fine, it's just …

She coughs.

BABS: [*offstage*] Theodora!
THEO: … burnt toast … sinuses … [*coughing*] your imagination.

Eyes frantic, she tries to devise a way to conceal the evidence.

BABS: [*offstage*] You don't sound 'fine' at all. You sound like trouble, young miss.

THEO *is at a loss. Desperate, she pours the ash into the back of the piano …*

Long beat.

[*Offstage*] I'm going out now.

THEO *throws up her hands, exasperated. The panic was all for nothing.*

[*Offstage*] Do you want me to pick you up a sweetie?

ACT ONE

No response.

[*Offstage*] Theodora ... Theodora?

    THEO *plonks herself down on the little stool and bows her head.*

[*Offstage*] Would you like a liquorice allsort?

    Beat.

[*Offstage*] Hello there, Theodora?

THEO: [*calling*] I'm okay, Mum. Have a good time!

    Beat.

BABS: [*offstage*] Alright, I'll pick you up a liquorice allsort.
THEO: [*under her breath*] Singular? Is this a famine?
BABS: Just a treat, between us girls!

    THEO *rubs her eyes.*

THEO: [*calling*] Thank you!

    She waits.

Has she gone? I think she's gone. She's the normal one. [*Depressed*] Fuck.

BABS: [*offstage*] Goodbye Theodora!
THEO: [*calling*] Goodbye!

    She waits again and then slowly withdraws a fresh joint and starts rolling it.

You can see why I have to leave, can't you? The worst part is, they're turning me into an arsehole. I don't *want* to be an ungrateful bitch. I don't want to shut them out. I don't want to be this brat who sulks all the time and hides from her family, and wears gingham in some kind of pitiful, self-shattering act of defiance. You see this? [*Waving her joint*] My father *likes* this. He thinks it makes me a rebel.

    Facepalm.

A 'rebel'? Christ on a stick, Dad! The sixties are over ... capitalism won.

    Big sigh.

He wants me to 'explore myself'. What's to explore? I'm pale, way too skinny, my body hair is a little weird, and I just want to be an accountant.

She takes another drag.

He says, 'Dope will open up your horizons, Theo'. But we all know that's another cliché, don't we? I just smoke it to ward off my anxiety. [*Smirking*] How fucktarded is that? I can't even be a normal tosser. I have to pioneer new ways to break from the past. Hence the gingham. Dad *hates* the gingham. He hates my politics too. Totally hates Hilary, calls her a 'sell-out'. Sometimes, when I really want to make a statement, I play Burt Bacharach on repeat … ooh yeah … [*grinning*] it kills him.

The lights start to flicker. THEO *looks up at them, heaving another sigh.*

You probably don't understand exactly where I'm coming from.

Wind howls.

Don't worry, you're about to.

Pink spots become flashes of electric blue lightning.

Snow drifts from the wings.

SCENE TWO

It's freezing out here. A white spot strikes centre stage where THEO *stands in a massive parka.* BARBARA *appears beside her in an even more elaborate outfit, somewhere between a ski instructor and an Eskimo. They're both shivering. The wind whips relentlessly.*

THEO: Well, this is bullshit.
BABS: What's that, dear?
THEO: *Bullshit!*

    The howling wind intensifies.

  Why didn't we go to Mount Hotham?
BABS: He'll be back any minute now.
THEO: What?
BABS: Beg pardon, dear?
THEO: I said, 'Why didn't we go to Mount Hotham?'

    BABS *checks her watch.*

BABS: Around half nine.

ACT ONE

THEO: Pardon?
BABS: What?

>Beat.

It's a little nippy, isn't it?
THEO: I can't feel my pinkie toe.
BABS: Enunciate, Theodora!
THEO: *My ... pinkie ... toe!*
BABS: I took a tinkle before we left!

> *Another figure appears, dressed in a Tibetan chuba (traditional long coat) with a hair sash, yak-skin boots, and prayer beads around his wrist. This is* THEO's *nightmare—this is* JASPER.

JASPER: This is glorious!
THEO: Fuck off, Dad!
JASPER: Don't you feel alive, Theo? I do! I feel … spiritual … I feel a sense of belonging, a sense of wholeness. Do you feel the wholeness?
THEO: It's not safe up here!
JASPER: 'Course it is! You just need to make contact with your primal self!
BABS: Speak up, love!
JASPER: *Primal ... seeeeelf!*
THEO: Dad, we have to turn around!
JASPER: Embrace your inner snow leopard!
THEO: Fucking what?!

> JASPER *pulls* THEO *downstage.*

JASPER: Look at the view, Theo. Can't you sense the magic?
THEO: My tits have frost bite!
JASPER: The Sherpa said that's normal!

> *The wind's howls become furious screams.*

THEO: Come on, we *have* to go!
JASPER: This is a divine experience!
BABS: You should be wearing an anorak, Jasper.
JASPER: Pardon?
BABS: *An anoooraaaaaaaaaaaaaak!*

> *The word echoes and echoes, and echoes.*
>
> *Blackout.*

SCENE THREE

Darkness.

ANNI: [*voiceover*] Ladies and gentlemen, welcome to Adelaide Airport. Local time is twelve p.m. and the temperature is a sunny twenty-eight degrees. For your safety and comfort, please remain seated with your seat belt fastened until the captain turns off the 'Fasten Seat Belt' sign. This will indicate that we have parked at the gate and it is safe for you to move about.

Music rises beneath the voice.

Please check around your seat for any personal belongings you may have brought onboard with you and please use caution when opening the overhead bins, as heavy articles may have shifted around during the flight.

The riff is instantly recognisable—'Sunshine of Your Love' (Cream). It begins to drown out the following:

We remind you to please wait until you are inside the terminal to use any electronic devices. On behalf of the captain and the entire crew, I'd like to thank you for joining us on this journey and we look forward to seeing you onboard again in the near future. Have a nice day.

Lights up.

We're back in the rock room. JASPER *is dancing to the music. He is now wearing a headband, leather jacket and boxer shorts.* THEO, *wearing a new gingham dress, watches her father with disdain.* BABS *is knitting, and smiling vacantly.*

The altar now displays an effigy of Shiva, the Auspicious One.

Musical notes appear around the walls, in time with the audio.

As the music grows louder, JASPER *sweeps* BABS *off her stool. They dance.* THEO *rolls her eyes.*

Beat.

JASPER *dips* BABS *and the two share a lingering kiss. With his free hand,* JASPER *offers* THEO *a joint.*

THEO: That's it!

> THEO *shuts off the CD player.*

Family conference!

> *Her parents deflate.*

BABS: Whatever is the matter with you, dear? You've been surly all week.

THEO: Sit down. Both of you.

JASPER: You're killing the vibe, Theo.

> *Beat.*

THEO: The 'vibe'?

JASPER: Yeah, the vibe, the spirit.

THEO: You're such a desperate wanker! [*Calming herself*] There is no vibe, Dad. I just want to have a civilised conversation with you.

BABS: Oh, that sounds very nice. Doesn't that sound nice, pet?

JASPER: [*to* THEO] You drain the energy from this room.

THEO: Five minutes.

JASPER: You suck it in. [*Gesturing*] This is my special space.

BABS: She's trying to assert herself. [*To* THEO] Go on, dear.

> THEO *opens her mouth to speak. Her father cuts her off.*

JASPER: I don't know why you have to be a downer all the time. [*To* BABS] Why can't she be more … up?

THEO: Five minutes, okay? Five whole minutes when it's not all about you, Dad.

JASPER: You should get streaks in your hair.

THEO: *Dad!*

> *Beat.*

> *They stare hard at each other.*

BABS: How about I put the kettle on?

THEO: No.

BABS: A little camomile might turn that frown into a giggle.

THEO: Sit your arse back down on the pouffe, Mother. I need to get this off my chest. It's sticking to me like phlegm.

JASPER: Don't you talk to her in that tone.

BABS: It's fine, love.

JASPER: [*to* THEO] Don't you dare! [*Appalled*] She's your life-giver.
THEO: Fuuuuck!
JASPER: You're totally killing the—

> THEO *explodes.*

THEO: If you say 'vibe' one more time I am going to shove your keytar so deep into your rectum that you'll be shitting in A minor for weeks!
BABS: Now that's just an absurd image.
THEO: I can't live like this.

> BABS *gives* JASPER *a sharp look. He takes the cue and adjusts his tone from confrontational to condescending.*

JASPER: You're growing up, becoming a woman … [*A big smile.*] I get it.
THEO: No! No, Dad … you *don't* get it. You think it's all daisies and acid trips.
JASPER: Let it out, Theo. We can take it.
THEO: Actually, it's even more tragic than that …
JASPER: Let us carry your pain.
THEO: You *pretend* to think like a flower child, but you're really just clinging to another time. Well, people grow up, Dad.
JASPER: And you need to actualise your personhood. Go ahead.

> *Beat.*

THEO: I enjoy folk music.
JASPER: That's your choice.
THEO: I enjoy vanilla sex.
BABS: Theodora!
THEO: Oooh … here's one for you, Dad …
JASPER: We don't have to be in conflict.
THEO: … I really dig mathematics. Yeah, it's the shiz. I fucking love it!

> *Long beat.*

JASPER: Just as we'll always love you, Theo.
THEO: Go to hell!

> *She storms downstage.*
>
> *A spotlight catches her, as her parents fade …*

SCENE FOUR

THEO *takes a second to compose herself.*

THEO: [*to the audience*] Don't say anything! I know that was pathetic. They turn me into such a whiner. Maybe I *am* a whiner. Jesusfuck, the last thing I want to be is a whiner. [*Calming down*] Deep breaths. Keep it in perspective … one and a half months. Just over six weeks. That's around forty-five days of oppression, right? I can cope with that.

Someone draws a sharp intake of breath from the back row, doubting THEO'*s words. A confident, chirpy voice calls out:*

ANNI: Oh, I dunno … can you?

THEO looks into the audience. She is genuinely miffed.

THEO: Excuse me?

ANNI: Well, you seem soooooo eager to get out there and make your mark on the world.

THEO: Is that sarcasm?

ANNI: [*upbeat*] I think so.

THEO: Maybe this world already has enough marks. Maybe I don't want to scar it any further.

Beat.

Are you done? Good. [*She sighs.*] Forty-five days. Not even four dozen sleeps. I can rally. It's doable.

Slowly, she finds her smile.

Sure it is. Cinch. Easy peasy. In fact, I've got backup!

A new spotlight appears. Inside sits THEO*'s boyfriend,* WALLACE, *his back to the audience.*

Have you met my boyfriend? He's a troll. I don't mean that in the derogatory sense … and I don't mean that in the fantastical sense either. He *is* a troll. Wallace spends at least three hours a day airing his grievances online.

She looks admiringly over at him.

Isn't he gorgeous?

WALLACE spins to face the audience as he types furiously on his laptop. He sports thick glasses, a flimsy T-shirt and a feeble goatee.

WALLACE: Fucking Abbott! Fucking wing nut, gherkin-dick cunt!

As he types, the words appear projected all around the flat.

THEO: [*with a wave*] Hello.

WALLACE: Oh, hi babe. [*Back to the net*] Go drink a litre of bleach you troglodyte scum! [*To* THEO] Can you believe how rude these conservatives are?

THEO: How was your day?

WALLACE: Well, Professor Taffy is on the warpath and my car keeps shitting itself.

THEO: Great. Listen, I want to move in with you.

WALLACE: I'm pretty sure the old couple upstairs have been stealing my mail again.

THEO: Did you catch what I just said?

WALLACE: They think I can't hear them laughing up there, but I so can.

THEO: Wallace …

WALLACE: I might slip a little camera between the stairs.

THEO: Honey, did you hear me?

WALLACE: Mmm?

THEO: I want to move in with you.

Beat.

WALLACE: Why?

THEO: Well … my parents …

WALLACE: Are you kidding? Your parents are fantastic!

THEO: [*dubious*] *My* parents?

WALLACE: They take you places.

THEO: Against my will.

WALLACE: But you've seen so much.

THEO: Are you avoiding the question?

WALLACE: You've been everywhere. All over the shop.

Awkward beat. He refuses to meet her eyes.

Tibet must have been amazing.

THEO: I got hypothermia.

WALLACE: [*too much*] And that was an experience!

ACT ONE 11

THEO: Wallace …
WALLACE: Yeah?
THEO: Don't you want me to stay?

He coughs.

WALLACE: It's just … you know, the timing …
THEO: [*frowning*] Timing?
WALLACE: Yeah, Abbott … the revolution …
THEO: Oh fuck.
WALLACE: What? What fuck?
THEO: I've just realised something cataclysmic. [*Pointing*] You!
WALLACE: Me?
THEO: You're just like him.
WALLACE: Just like who?
THEO: My father!
WALLACE: No.
THEO: Yes!
WALLACE: [*dismissive*] No, no, no, not at all …
THEO: You are and you know it!

Beat.

WALLACE: Well, he's quite inspirational.

THEO *lets out a shriek.* WALLACE *is a little scared.*

Things must be really bad at home.
THEO: I just want to be ordinary!
WALLACE: Ordinary? Come on, Theo.
THEO: What's wrong with ordinary?
WALLACE: Everyone is a unique and special creature.
THEO: That's a steaming heap of crap!
WALLACE: Look, I have stuff to do here so—
THEO: That's the turd they squeeze into a plastic tube and shove down our throats when we're children.
WALLACE: You're obviously not in a cheerful place right now.
THEO: You know those tubes? The thin ones?
WALLACE: I was really hoping for some nookie.
THEO: They shove them in while we're learning to talk and pump their foul sludge into our guts … [*beating her chest*] into our hearts!

WALLACE: [*deadpan*] And I will not be having a delicious lunch today.
THEO: They poison our insides … [*menacing*] with shit.

Beat.

WALLACE: [*walking her out*] Yeah, no, that last comment was a real mood-killer.

THEO *stands her ground.*

Beat.

THEO: Wallace, even if you are one in a million, you're still just ordinary. There are seven *billion* people in the world now, did you know that?
WALLACE: [*sighing*] Okay, I'm going in. [*With forced patience*] You choose not to exercise your voice, and I acknowledge that … it's cool … it's peachy. However, my path—
THEO: I *will* bite you, Wallace.
WALLACE: No, no, listen … my path is the path of the social thinker. Like Socrates, or … or … who's that guy from Texas?

THEO *bites his arm.*

Argh! [*Remembering*] Dr Phil!

They're both panting, out of breath.

THEO: You're in denial. [*Correcting herself*] You're a dick and you're in denial.
WALLACE: I really have to work, Theo. [*Suddenly hopeful*] Unless you're feeling affectionate?
THEO: I'm not.
WALLACE: Then our business is concluded.
THEO: [*with thick sarcasm*] You're a prince.
WALLACE: I'm sorry I couldn't be more helpful.

She turns to leave.

Theo, wait.

He fishes inside his laptop bag and withdraws a book.

This literature might set you on a different path.
THEO: [*reading*] Eat, Pray, Love.

Beat.

She whacks him over the head with the book. Once. Twice. As long as it takes to vent her frustration.

ACT ONE 13

WALLACE: Theo!

He cowers and then watches her go, shaking his head.

Little lost soul.

SCENE FIVE

Projected image: Susan Boyle singing 'I Dreamed a Dream'. The image dissolves into JASPER, *playing piano and singing in time with her, sadly. Occasionally he sips from a glass of whiskey, which is perched on his piano.*

Musical notes appear. Some shatter or wilt, depending on the mood and pitch.

THEO *enters*.

THEO: Oh no. Boyle.

She gives him a little wave.

Hey Dad.
JASPER: It's over, Theo.
THEO: What's over?
JASPER: The dream.

He sips.

The dream is over.
THEO: I'm really tired. Can we just ... *not* have a crisis tonight?
JASPER: I was a star once. A shooting star.
THEO: Please don't bring out the reviews.

It's too late. JASPER *holds up a yellowing newspaper.*

JASPER: [*reading*] 'Jasper Sprout has an enviable vocal range.' [*Nodding*] He said 'enviable' ... he *envied* me ...
THEO: You had your moment, Dad. Nobody can take that away.
JASPER: Who would envy me now, Theo?
THEO: I'm going to bed.

THEO *tries to leave.* JASPER *calls after her.*

JASPER: [*reading*] 'Sprout has Eddie Vedder's pipes and Elvis Presley's hips.' [*Pointing*] That's a young Elvis, mind you.
THEO: I know that, Dad.

JASPER: That's not a tubby Elvis.
THEO: I know! May I please go to bed?

> *Beat.*

> *She makes another attempt to get out of there.*

JASPER: I remember when we took you home from the hospital. Our little bundle of crazy.
THEO: [*slumping*] Alright, I'll put the kettle on.
JASPER: You used to look up to me then. I could see it in your eyes. What happened to your eyes, Theo?

> *He takes another sip of whiskey and plays 'Cat's in the Cradle' on the piano.*

> THEO *makes a cup of tea.*

THEO: White? With two?

> JASPER *doesn't hear her. He's too busy humming along to his tune.*

Dad?

> *He stops playing.*

JASPER: What's it all about, Theo? Why are we here?
THEO: We're not doing this.
JASPER: I just want some—
THEO: Applause?
JASPER: —meaning. I want … I *need* … a purpose.
THEO: Have a cup of tea.

> *This breaks* JASPER *from his dark mood. He looks over at* THEO *and softens.*

JASPER: You sound just like your mother.
THEO: [*smiling*] Shut your face.

> *She passes him the cup.*

JASPER: Ta.

> *Beat.*

> *It's the first warm moment they've shared. Naturally, he screws it up completely.*

Sit down. There's something I want to share with you. I've been reading about this swami in Bengal.

ACT ONE

THEO: No.
JASPER: Don't shut me down offhand.
THEO: We're not going to Bengal.
JASPER: But the man is a revelation.
THEO: I don't care.
JASPER: Theo, you shouldn't close yourself to new experiences.
THEO: [*eyes to the ceiling*] Why didn't I just go to bed?
JASPER: It's powerful stuff. He has discovered the essence of spiritual harmonisation.

He tries to draw her close. THEO *shakes him away.*

THEO: *What the hell is your problem, Dad?!*
JASPER: …
THEO: Are Mum and I so deficient that you have to keep chasing your own tail around the globe searching for … for … fuck, I don't even know what you think you're missing!
JASPER: That's why I have to find it.
THEO: This house is full of your toys. [*Pointing*] That piano could cover my HECS debt!
JASPER: So what? It's just *stuff*. It can't nourish me.
THEO: You're a spoilt, stubborn old—

BABS *enters in her nightgown, clutching a hot water bottle.*

BABS: Theodora!
THEO: It's not me! He's in a mood.
BABS: [*frowning*] How bad?
THEO: Boyle bad!
BABS: Heavens. [*A light bulb moment.*] Did you put the kettle on?
THEO: Kill me.

JASPER *downs his glass of whiskey in a half-second.*

JASPER: Babs, we're going to Kolkata!
BABS: Kolkata? Where's that, dear?
THEO: [*with a sigh*] Bengal.
BABS: Bengal?
JASPER: Bengal!
THEO: We have jobs, Dad! We have commitments!
BABS: Is it nice in Bengal?

THEO: [*to* BABS] You don't have to support him. [*To* JASPER, *gently as she can*] Dad, it's time you made peace with your life.

JASPER: …

THEO: It's not all about how many people you know, or who writes about you, or who recognises you on the street.

JASPER: Some people are meant to stand up and shine, Theo.

BABS: Oh, kettle's boiling!

THEO: You don't need public recognition. Just be nice to the neighbours, give a little to charity …

BABS: I'll get the cups out, shall I?

THEO: Just be a good husband and a good father.

JASPER: [*scoffing*] Who is going to notice that?

> *Long beat.*
>
> BABS *is frozen, cups in hand. She looks nervously from her husband to her daughter and back again.*

THEO: [*icy*] Fuck you, Dad.

> JASPER *swallows.*

JASPER: I'm sorry you're so conventional.

> JASPER *exits.*
>
> BABS *pours tea in the heavy silence.*

BABS: He didn't mean that.

THEO: Yeah, he did.

BABS: Your father has very high expectations of himself.

> THEO *accepts her cup.*

THEO: Mum, we've got to stop doing this.

BABS: Doing what, darling?

THEO: We've got to stop travelling the world with that maniac.

> *She passes the cup back.*

BABS: Not thirsty?

> THEO *shakes her head. She's fighting to hold in tears.*

THEO: Smells funny.

BABS: It's one of my favourites. Sleepytime.

THEO: [*with a sniff*] M'sorry, Mum. [*In a little voice*] Why is he so mean?

ACT ONE

BABS: Oh dear, please don't cry. If you cry, I'll shatter.

> *She pulls* THEO *into a hug.*

He appreciates you. Truly, he does. You're all he talks about.

THEO: *He's* all he talks about.

> *Beat.*

Mum?

BABS: Yes, darling?

THEO: I'm … I'm going to chunder!

> *She rushes over to the piano.*

BABS: Not there!

> *They both freeze as the lights turn a sickly green.*
>
> *Beat.*
>
> THEO *breaks out of the freeze.* BABS *continues to stand immobile.*

THEO: Dad would call this an 'emotional purge'.

> *From the back row, a familiar voice pipes up.*

ANNI: But it's not all for him.

> ANESIDORA SPROUT *strides to the stage. She has* THEO*'s frosted blonde hair and a darker shade of gingham in her skirt. If* THEO *were tougher and less conservative the two might be twins.*

You need to start putting yourself first, Theo.

THEO: [*wincing*] Isn't that what I've been doing?

ANNI: No, you've been moaning like a limpdick. Nobody likes a limpdick, Theo. It's time you expressed yourself.

THEO: Who *are* you?

ANNI: Anni.

THEO: [*nonplussed*] Anni?

ANNI: Anesidora.

> *She extends her hand.*

THEO: Wow. Your parents are sadder than mine.

ANNI: [*with a smirk*] That's a fact.

> THEO *groans and bends over. She's close to being sick.* ANNI *withdraws her hand.*

I couldn't just watch all of this play out. Had to say something.

She approaches BABS, *who is still frozen stiff.*

Family dramas are so … pedestrian.

THEO *gags.*

THEO: [*between shudders*] Well—that's—the—point.

ANNI *circles* BABS *and waves her hand in front of her eyes.* BABS *doesn't react.*

ANNI: Yes, yes, you want to be ordinary. We all caught that. The thing is, Theo … and I'm sure you're aware of this … being ordinary is really just a defence mechanism.

THEO: [*recovering*] It really isn't.

ANNI: You don't think so? Interesting.

Grinning like a wildcat, ANNI *withdraws purple lipstick from her pocket and smears it all over* BABS' *lips.*

I think you are a coward.

THEO: [*darkly*] A coward?

ANNI: Mmmm. You say you *want* to be ordinary and the world forgives you when that's all you manage to achieve. It's a … what's the expression … logical fallacy?

She thinks, snaps her fingers.

No, a propositional fallacy. Ordinary *or* extraordinary, exceptional or unexceptional. Has it not occurred to you that one can be both?

She steps back to admire her work.

Sexy, isn't she?

THEO: What?

ANNI: She's sexy.

THEO: She's my mother.

ANNI: And she's sexy.

THEO: Look, I think you should sit back do—

ANNI *spins to face* THEO. *Immediately,* THEO *doubles over in pain.*

ANNI: You're not well. I'll give you a second to catch up. Three guesses? No? [*Calling*] Wallace!

WALLACE *enters.* ANNI *vanishes.*

SCENE SIX

WALLACE *is wearing embarrassing pyjamas—comic book or sci-fi themed. His hair is all over the place.* THEO *stares at him.*

WALLACE: What the hell are you shouting for? You could just text me. I need my rest, Theo!

THEO: …

>*He clocks her look and covers his pyjamas with his dressing-gown.*

WALLACE: I asked you not to come here after dark, didn't I? If the lady down the hall decides to lodge another complaint, I'm royally screwed.

THEO: I'm late.

WALLACE: I know you're late.

>*He checks watch.*

Man, it's nearly four!

THEO: No … Wallace, I'm *late*.

>*He waves his wristwatch—also comic book or sci-fi themed—in her face.*

WALLACE: I *know!*

>*Beat.*

>*She can't believe what's she's dealing with.*

THEO: Alright, let's start again. Do you remember that night up at the shack?

WALLACE: Grandpa's shack?

THEO: That's the one.

WALLACE: Sure, I remember.

THEO: And I wore the … the thing?

WALLACE: The Princess Leia slave bikini?

THEO: [*with a sigh*] We're gonna have to change that story.

WALLACE: It was awesome.

THEO: [*to herself*] I'll come up with something more romantic.

WALLACE: Best night ever.

THEO: Something less sad.

WALLACE: Why are we talking about this?
THEO: Because!

   Beat.

Jesus, Wallace … how are you not getting this? We went to bed, yeah?
WALLACE: [*nodding*] Grandpa's bed.
THEO: And we were … intimate.
WALLACE: [*under his breath*] Don't tell Grandpa.
THEO: And then something sprung a leak and you cried.
WALLACE: I did *not* cry. It was just an expression of … momentary unease. I mean, imagine if you'd fallen pregnant.
THEO: Hallelujah!
WALLACE: Eh?
THEO: Give the boy a gumdrop!
WALLACE: Theo, what are you talking about?
THEO: *We leaked! I'm pregnant!*

   Beat.

WALLACE: With a baby?
THEO: No Wallace, with a St. Bernard. Are you going to let me in or would you prefer we starve to death on your doorstep?
WALLACE: How did this happen?
THEO: Seriously? I just took you through it!
WALLACE: [*pointing*] There's another person in there?
THEO: There's a … little piece of person in here. Kinda like a goldfish.
WALLACE: But you said 'we'! You just said 'we'!
THEO: That's right, Wallace … it's gonna grow up and it's gonna get hungry. Now, can we please take this conversation inside? You don't want the neighbours to know you've been splashing your seed around town, do you?
WALLACE: I haven't been splashing! *You* deflowered *me*, Theodora!
THEO: You bought the outfit! [*She thinks.*] Wait a second … that really was your first time? Wow, you sure made it count.
WALLACE: Shit.
THEO: I know.
WALLACE: Shit!
THEO: I know!

ACT ONE 21

Dogs bark.

Long beat.

I'm sorry. [*Smiling weakly*] I could've done this in a more ... delicate way.

WALLACE: [*listening*] We've upset the Pomeranians.

THEO: Who?

He points to the floor above.

Right. Look, we don't have to make any decisions just now. [*With a shrug*] It's a goldfish.

WALLACE: You don't want to be a mother?

THEO: Do you want to be a father?

WALLACE: ...

THEO: Exactly.

Beat.

WALLACE: I don't suppose I can engineer vital social change while I'm changing nappies and ... [*shrugging*] coaching soccer.

THEO: You don't know how to play soccer.

WALLACE: I so do! That's the one with the chessboard ball!

THEO: But it's not like chess ...

WALLACE: *I think you're wrong about that!*

She frowns at him. He calms himself.

Sorry, sorry, this is just ... grown-up.

THEO: We need to stay level.

WALLACE: [*nodding*] Level.

THEO: No fast decisions.

WALLACE: My life plan was clear: major in political science, topple government, guest star on *Q&A*.

THEO: Wallace, you're not a revolutionary.

WALLACE: I so am!

He points to his beard.

Look at my Lenin patch.

THEO *hangs her head.*

THEO: How could I screw someone so brainfucked?

WALLACE: I have a Che Guevara T-shirt on special order too.

THEO: Come here.

They kiss.

WALLACE: Alright, let's go inside and talk like proper grown-ups.
THEO: Oh God no. We've got to do better than that.

Blackout.

SCENE SEVEN

In the darkness, muzak plays. It is saccharine, 'life-affirming' and vaguely spiritual.

CHAD: [*voiceover*] Are you feeling hollow? Are you searching for a new path? Does the world around you feel cold and spiritually bankrupt? Well … let's take a walk.

Lights rise slowly on CHAD MOMBARDO. *He's snazzily dressed, too plastic, and too tanned.*

[*To the audience*] Good evening, ladies and gentleman. No, don't get up. My name is Chad Mombardo and I'm here to expand you.

He snaps his fingers and the lights become gently floating stars.

Have you ever found yourself yearning for something more? Have you ever, truly, found yourself? These questions are a beginning … and a beginning, my friends, is a promise you make with your heart. If you find yourself asking, seeking, promising, then you are one of the special ones. You are one of the sacred few.

The muzak develops into a throbbing beat. CHAD's *tempo increases. He is casting his spell.*

I don't deal with cattle. No, I'm not a farmer! I don't have time for those who wander through life with their eyes glazed. I'm here to support the winners, the choosers. I believe I was put on this earth to coach champions!

He removes his jacket to reveal a T-shirt with a flaming peace symbol.

With my twelve step syllabus I can show you the way forward. I can take you by the hand … [*leaning into the audience, touching flesh*] and guide you to that new job, new boy, new toy. I can enrich your spirit and nourish your fundamental exceptionalness. [*Pointing*] Do you want to grab tomorrow by the short and silkies? I can help you!

The muzak climaxes.

But wait!

He gestures. The muzak drops.

You want a demonstration, right? Well, of course you do! And I want a guinea pig!

JASPER: [*eagerly, from the audience*] Hey, man, over here!

CHAD: What's that I spy? Could it be a willing sacrifice? Step on up, my friend. [*To the audience*] Let's give this clown a hand!

A spotlight falls on JASPER. *He rushes to* CHAD*'s side, wearing a big, dopey, lapdog grin.*

Tell everyone who you are.

JASPER *speaks confidently into* CHAD*'s microphone.*

JASPER: Jasper.

CHAD: Jasper!

JASPER: Jasper Sprout.

CHAD: Now there's a name that grows on you! Tell me, Jasper ... tell me for realsies ... is your life all you ever dreamed it could be? Or is there something missing? Have you noticed ... gaps?

JASPER: Gaps?

CHAD: Happiness gaps? Achievement gaps? [*Winding up the crowd*] Yearnings unfulfilled?

JASPER: I ... I miss my work.

CHAD: Have you lost your job, Jasper?

JASPER: I used to sing.

He looks down at his toes.

I used to be good.

CHAD*'s eyes practically morph into dollar signs.*

CHAD: Step One: What's Past Is Prologue ... Your greatest accomplishments lie ahead.

Many of CHAD*'s buzzwords and phrases float around them as they speak. The letters drift like fumes, infecting* JASPER.

JASPER: [*hopeful*] Do you mean that?

CHAD: I mean it if *you* mean it!
JASPER: [*grinning*] I mean it!
CHAD: Give this champ a button!

> *A* STAGE HAND *hurries over and sticks a badge on* JASPER. *It is the same flaming peace sign that* CHAD *wears.*

This is your beginning: your promise to you. Oh, you'll sing again, Jasper Sprout. You'll burn the house down!

> *He throws his arm over* JASPER. *The wolf has found a fresh piece of meat.*

All it will take is eleven more steps.

> *A phone rings.*

SCENE EIGHT

WALLACE *emerges from under a quilt. He searches around his bedroom for his screeching phone.* THEO *remains out cold, snoring audibly.*

THEO: [*between snores*] The squirrel ...
WALLACE: Huh?
THEO: ... he's singing ...
WALLACE: You're okay, Theo. It's only a dream.
THEO: Make him stop.
WALLACE: I'm working on it.

> *At last, the phone is found.* WALLACE *checks the number. A spotlight appears, stage left, to reveal* FIGSBY. *She's young, black, athletic, self-assured ... and dressed in a onesie.*

Figsby?
FIGSBY: Where were you, Wallace?
WALLACE: I was here ... [*Frowning*] Where was I supposed to be?
FIGSBY: We had a meeting!
WALLACE: That was tonight?
FIGSBY: There was a crowd of people waiting to hear you speak!
WALLACE: A crowd, really?
FIGSBY: [*recalculating*] There was a crowd of *seven* people waiting to hear you speak!

> WALLACE *deflates.*

ACT ONE 25

WALLACE: I'm sorry.
FIGSBY: How can we have a revolution if you keep forgetting to show up?
WALLACE: It won't happen again.
FIGSBY: I made fruit punch! The tangy one you like!
WALLACE: Bring it over tomorrow.
FIGSBY: It's all spoiled!
WALLACE: Look, I'm … I'm having a bad week.

He glances anxiously over at THEO.

FIGSBY: [*to herself*] He's having a bad week … [*Shaking her head*] *Jesus!*
WALLACE: Well, I am! [*In a hushed tone*] There's a girl here.

FIGSBY'*s attitude transforms instantly from frustrated to thrilled.*

FIGSBY: A girl?
WALLACE: Yeah, a … you know …

WALLACE *cups his hand over the receiver, sharing his secret like a giggly school kid.*

… a special lady friend.
FIGSBY: [*grinning*] Why are you talking to me? Get back into bed!
WALLACE: I'm just gonna grab a glass of water.
FIGSBY: Get back into bed and thank the angels!
WALLACE: I'm a little parched.
FIGSBY: Get back into bed and show her the moves.
WALLACE: The moves?
FIGSBY: Yeah, the moves … she's gotta see them …

She starts gyrating her hips, dancing on the spot.

A bit of this … and a bit of …
WALLACE: I don't know what you're doing.
FIGSBY: Slowly, you don't wanna rush it.
WALLACE: You do realise we're on the telephone?
FIGSBY: Just steer it, steer it …
WALLACE: Steer? Steer what? She's doesn't have an engine, she's a mammal.
FIGSBY: Be gentle, be respectful, she's a lady … and then … twist …
WALLACE: I have no idea what you're talking about. No clue.

FIGSBY *deflates.*

FIGSBY: Shit, I keep forgetting that you're white.
WALLACE: I can change! [*Grinning sheepishly*] I really fancy this girl.
FIGSBY: [*with thick sarcasm*] That's great. Talk about your feelings.
WALLACE: Don't be like that. I can learn. I can be … primal.
FIGSBY: Primal? No, not you, princess.

The phone beeps.

WALLACE: Hang on a sec, I've got another call coming in.

Lights appear, stage right, to reveal SASHA. *Livid. Ready to maim. She is sitting up in bed with rollers in her flame-red hair and her toes darkly polished and drying. A teddy is tucked under one hand while a cigarette dangles from the other.*

SASHA: *Wallace, you big tampon!*
WALLACE: Okay, I know I let everyone down, but there's a good rea—
SASHA: *Shove it!* Shove it in deep! We put our faith in you!
WALLACE: I get that.
SASHA: We put you on the top of our ticket!
WALLACE: If you'll just … *try* to develop some empathy …

Not a great choice of words. SASHA *erupts.*

SASHA: *Don't give me orders, you parrot-faced hobgoblin!*
WALLACE: [*stung*] Troll. I'm a troll.
SASHA: The people rallied! We brought chips!
WALLACE: I'm sorry, alright? I'm sorry, I'm sorry, I'm sorry!

Beat.

SASHA *finally takes a breather, and then a long drag.*

Are you smoking in bed again?
SASHA: This is your fault. You made me tense.
WALLACE: Promise you'll put it out before you turn in.
SASHA: Ah, so you *do* care?
WALLACE: Promise me, Sash. You might not make it out alive next time.
FIGSBY: Hey, Sasha, you'll never believe this …

WALLACE *looks down at his phone.*

WALLACE: Aww, balls … she's still here.
FIGSBY: Wallace has a girl in his bed! A *real* one!

ACT ONE

SASHA: Did the inflatable one finally disintegrate?
WALLACE: My romantic life should not be a source of mirth. You're both supposed to respect me.

They burst out laughing.

SASHA: Is she fat? She has to be fat!
WALLACE: That's really superficial and uncalled for.
SASHA: Is she humongous?
WALLACE: No!
SASHA: [*sitting up, deadly serious*] Oh God, is she blind?
WALLACE: Sash!
FIGSBY: Alright, here's a tip: you need to think of it as a war.
WALLACE: [*with a nod*] War.
FIGSBY: A sexy war.
WALLACE: Sexy war. Nice.
FIGSBY: She doesn't want you to surrender.
WALLACE: I will not surrender.
FIGSBY: She wants you to conquer.

WALLACE makes an animal growl.

SASHA: Don't do that.
WALLACE: Sorry.
FIGSBY: If she gets hot, if you feel the fire between you … embrace her …
WALLACE: Embrace her!
FIGSBY: Take her in your arms and you will be victorious!
WALLACE: *Victorious!*

THEO snores. WALLACE jumps back in fright.

Beat. His voice returns to a whisper.

Is that not a little offensive?
SASHA: Mate, tear the barcode from your penis, shake off the bubble wrap and give it a twirl.
WALLACE: You don't know what I've achieved, Sasha! Okay? You don't know the trouble my … my … [*looking down*] friend has caused.

THEO rolls over, dreaming …

THEO: [*asleep*] Did you put the kittens in the mayonnaise?

WALLACE: It's alright, honey. Everything's good. [*Back into the phone*] I'll call you both tomorrow.

FIGSBY: *Viva la revolution!*

   Beat.

WALLACE: Yep.

   He hangs up. FIGSBY *and* SASHA *vanish.*

   WALLACE *crawls back into bed with* THEO, *careful not to wake her.* THEO *turns in her sleep and spoons him.*

   Lights fade.

SCENE NINE

BABS: [*offstage*] Have you taken the rubbish out?

   A bedside lamp illuminates JASPER, *sleepy-eyed. He wraps himself tight in his dressing-gown and kicks his feet into a pair of slippers.*

I did mention it earlier.

JASPER: I know you did.

BABS: [*offstage*] And mind that you turn them around the right way. There was a very unpleasant letter stuck to the yellow bin last week. I don't think they'll warn us again.

JASPER: I'll be meticulous.

   He shuffles away.

BABS: Dear …

   Another bedside lamp switches on, revealing BABS, *clutching a hot water bottle. She gestures to the little bin beside their bed.*

You'll need to empty this one too. It's full of your toenail clippings.

   He picks up the bin and stares into it.

Jasper?

   Beat.

Darling, are you ill?

JASPER: [*with a big sigh*] This isn't glamorous.

BABS: Hurry up and empty it before your side gets chilly.

She pats the bed. He heaves another sigh and heads off.
Beat.
He returns.

JASPER: I can't.
BABS: Of course you can, just tip them into the garden.
JASPER: No, I ... [*He exhales.*] I need more.
BABS: ...
JASPER: I need to *be* more.
BABS: [*worried*] More than what we have?
JASPER: More than the sad, decrepit, toenail clipping guy.

BABS knows he's serious, but tries to lighten the mood anyway.

BABS: Oh petal, are you having a sulk? Why don't you pray to Shiva and—
JASPER: Shiva's in the yellow bin. It wasn't working out between us.
BABS: [*pointing*] Well, who is that then?

JASPER glances at the altar.

JASPER: That's Apollo. He's into music.
BABS: Why isn't he wearing any trousers?
JASPER: That's the way he came in the post.
BABS: Well, it's unnerving. He has a look about him.
JASPER: A look?
BABS: He's a little too proud of his 'area'.
JASPER: [*taking a peek*] He should be.

BABS shakes her head.

BABS: I thought the last vision quest would be enough, but it's all a loop with you, isn't it? Every day is another deity.

Beat.

Am *I* the problem? Do you feel like you need an escape from our marriage?
JASPER: Come on, Babs ...
BABS: You'd tell me, wouldn't you? Because I don't want to be a millstone around your neck.
JASPER: You're not.
BABS: I'd rather be a divorcée. I could move to Florida like one of the Golden Girls.

JASPER: I swear, it's not you.
BABS: Then what is it?

> *He sits on the edge of the bed.*

JASPER: I thought I'd be further along by now. Life is a journey, right? Well, I thought I'd be onto the exciting bit. Instead I'm stuck at base camp.
BABS: Paul McCartney said 'Life is what happens when you're busy making other plans.'
JASPER: That was John Lennon. Paul said, 'Live and let die.' Fuck Paul.

> BABS *takes his hand.*

BABS: I'm sorry that you're disappointed, but please remember that it's *my* life too. And Theodora's.
JASPER: Theo will make her own life. I'll be a guest star at best.

> *Beat.*

I'm such a fuckup.
BABS: [*gently*] Put the bins out and come back to bed.

> *He nods and does as he's told.*

> BABS *waits for him to go, then smooths her hair down, undoes her top button and checks herself out in the bedside mirror.*

> *Beat.*

> *She returns to the bed and strikes a seductive pose.*

> *Another beat. Something feels wrong.*

> *She hurries over to Apollo and turns him around so that he is facing the wall.*

Better.

> *Beat.*

> *She covers him with a tea cosy.*

Much better.

> *Beat.*

Pervert.

> *She returns to the bed.*

> *Lights crossfade.*

ACT ONE

SCENE TEN

Lights up on THEO, *tangled in bed sheets. An alarm clock wails—more Susan Boyle.*

THEO: Arggh! I'll get up in a minute, Mum.

Her hand rises feebly and slaps at the clock until it dies.

Mum?

ANNI appears in a spotlight. She is rocking a brand new dress.

ANNI: You know what the difference is between you and me? [*Winking*] I make gingham look good.

She does a twirl.

THEO: Dammit ... I'd hoped you were a hallucination.

ANNI: [*air kissing*] I love you too.

*Grinning—always grinning—*ANNI *snatches* THEO *by the hand and drags her out of bed.*

Wakey wakey! Rise and stumble!

Bright lights.

THEO *is reluctant to stir.*

THEO: [*sleepy*] Five more minutes?

She squints under the lights. An easel appears.

ANNI: You've been dozing through life for far too long. It's time to get your hands dirty.

ANNI *throws a smock over* THEO *and shoves a paintbrush in her hand.*

THEO: Forget it.
ANNI: Indulge me.
THEO: I don't know how to paint
ANNI: Elephants paint. Think of it as a mirror.

She forces THEO *to look at the blank canvas.*

What do you see?
THEO: Nothing.
ANNI: Big fibber. [*Holding her head*] What do you see?

THEO: *Nothing!*

> *She wriggles away from* ANNI.

Art doesn't hold a mirror up to life … art holds a mirror up to art. It's a closed circle.

ANNI: Elephants never forget. [*Teasing*] You need to leave something behind for the people yet to become. How else will the world remember you, Theodora Sprout?

THEO: It won't have to. Don't you get it? I'm not a show pony. [*Angry*] I'm not my father!

ANNI: Take that rage and paint it.

THEO: Get off.

ANNI: Your father isn't here. What do you see?

THEO: Get off!

ANNI: What do you—?

THEO: *Me!*

> *She raises the brush. Music rises—a dissonant combination of rock and electropop—anything from Jefferson Airplane's 'White Rabbit' to Sophie Ellis-Bextor purring 'Heartbreak (Make me a dancer)', or Gorillaz, or Hendrix, or even the Pet Shop Boys, as* ANNI's *world takes over.*
>
> THEO *starts painting furiously. It isn't a coherent image, it doesn't have to be, but she loses herself in it.*
>
> *Enter the six* CRITICS. *Each of them is flamboyantly dressed—peacocks strutting for approval—and cartoonish in their voice and movements. They all wear rose-tinted glasses and traces of gingham here and there: gingham ties, gingham belts, gingham ribbons. Strobe lights herald their arrival.*
>
> ANNI *receives a glass of pink champagne from the* FIRST CRITIC *and joins their circle.*

FIRST CRITIC: A revelation! Simply … revealing!

THIRD CRITIC: So revealing!

ALL CRITICS: *A triumph!*

> *The critics sip their glasses together in perfect synchronisation.*

SECOND CRITIC: Note the red.

FIRST CRITIC: Ah yes, the red!

> *A giant red gingham square appears.*

FOURTH CRITIC: Menstrual blood.
SIXTH CRITIC: Oh, I see that!
THIRD CRITIC: How could you not?
FIRST CRITIC: The last cry of childhood / before the next step.
FOURTH CRITIC: Before the woman appears.
FIRST CRITIC: Obviously.
FOURTH CRITIC: [*nodding*] Obviously.
SIXTH CRITIC: And yet …
THIRD CRITIC: Yet?
SIXTH CRITIC: Why be so / restrained?
FOURTH CRITIC: Restrained by convention. Yes, I see that now.
SECOND CRITIC: And why be so literal / when the work is …
THIRD CRITIC: Literal, yes. It's the feeling that / hums.
FIFTH CRITIC: Sings.
FIRST CRITIC: It *does* sing, doesn't it?
SECOND CRITIC: … abstract?
FOURTH CRITIC: Intangible. Quite.
SIXTH CRITIC: I see / that.
FIRST CRITIC: I see that now.
SECOND CRITIC: But what do you suppose she is / feeling?
FIRST CRITIC: Anger … or passion, perhaps?
FOURTH CRITIC: But why be / literal?
SECOND CRITIC: Yes, why be literal?
FOURTH CRITIC: Quite.

> *They ponder.*
>
> *Beat.*

ANNI: Of course, one cannot take the red in isolation.

> *The critics burst into another passionate babble.*

FIRST CRITIC: [*nodding*] One *cannot* / take the red in isolation.
FOURTH CRITIC: One can*not*.
SECOND CRITIC: *Must* not.

> *A giant blue gingham square appears.*

FIFTH CRITIC: Breathtaking.
FIRST CRITIC: [*touching her heart*] Melancholy.
SECOND CRITIC: Beautiful. But it's a sad / beauty.
FOURTH CRITIC: A gentle beauty.
FIFTH CRITIC: I can see / that.
SIXTH CRITIC: I can see that clearly.
SECOND CRITIC: Quite.
FOURTH CRITIC: Quite.

   Beat.

ANNI: A cry for help, wouldn't you all agree?

   The critics turn their heads in perfect synchronisation.

FIRST CRITIC: A cry for / solace.
THIRD CRITIC: For a better / tomorrow.
FIFTH CRITIC: For a life free / of regret.
SECOND CRITIC: A happy life, free—yes—of regret.

   Beat.

   ANNI *is enjoying herself.*

ANNI: A post-post-modern expression of our / contemporary society.
SECOND CRITIC: Our / great society.
THIRD CRITIC: Our damaged / society.
FOURTH CRITIC: Society.
FIRST CRITIC: Society / indeed.
SECOND CRITIC: Indeed.
SIXTH CRITIC: Oh, indeed.
FIFTH CRITIC: And so relevant.
FOURTH CRITIC: Sooo relevant.
ALL CRITICS: *Inspiring!*

   Beat.

   A giant black and white gingham square appears.

ANNI: And the white?

   She looks at them with a sly smile. They just can't help themselves.

FIFTH CRITIC: The void!
FIRST CRITIC: Ooh, the void!
THIRD CRITIC: The void we all feel in our / hearts.

SECOND CRITIC: In our / bones.
FOURTH CRITIC: In our / minds.
THIRD CRITIC: Our souls.
FIRST CRITIC: The void, darling.
THIRD CRITIC: The void!
FOURTH CRITIC: And yet ...
FIFTH CRITIC: Yet?
SIXTH CRITIC: It's about absence.
FOURTH CRITIC: ... there is hope.
SECOND CRITIC: It's about longing / which is what makes the work so ...
FIRST CRITIC: The Freudian deficiency that all women / suffer.
FIFTH CRITIC: All minorities suffer.
SECOND CRITIC: ... vital.
FIRST CRITIC: Soooo vital!
SIXTH CRITIC: With the ...
FOURTH CRITIC: And the ...
THIRD CRITIC: Of course!
SECOND CRITIC: So much ...
FIFTH CRITIC: Sooooooo much!
ALL CRITICS: *Extraordinary!*

THEO throws her paintbrush down and glares at them.

THEO: It's a coloured square. [*Fiercely*] They're all just coloured squares!

Beat.

The critics down their glasses in perfect synchronisation.

ALL CRITICS: Oh.

They freeze. Slowly, the lights fade on them. They exit.

Music dies.

THEO faces ANNI.

THEO: What are you trying to prove?
ANNI: That we're the same, Theo. You can't just be—
THEO: Yes, I can! I can just *be*. I don't need to be laminated or published, or scrutinised, or dissected. I can just live. The moment is enough.
ANNI: But don't you hunger for significance?
THEO: For an audience, you mean? No, I really don't.
ANNI: [*stung*] There has to be more to you than this.

THEO: I'm sorry. This is all I am.
ANNI: *Fibber!*

> *Petulant and ungracious, like a child who has had their favourite toy snatched away,* ANNI *turns on her heel and runs offstage.*

> THEO *stares after her.*

THEO: Anni, wait. [*Calling*] Anni!

> *She falls back onto the bed.*
> *Lights change.*

SCENE ELEVEN

THEO *sits up to find* WALLACE, *hammering away on his lappy.*

WALLACE: Good morning, sweetness and light. Do you know how to spell 'ignoramus'?
THEO: That's an ironic question. [*Rubbing her eyes*] Tell me I didn't sleep over.
WALLACE: [*grinning*] We spooned.
THEO: Aww fucksticks.

> *He resumes his typing. She buries her face in a pillow.*

WALLACE: Did you have a nightmare?
THEO: How can you tell?
WALLACE: You were screaming at the lamp. [*With a shrug*] I thought I'd let you sleep in for a bit. *The Bolt Report* was on so I snuck out to vomit at the TV.

> *She sits up again, feeling her chest.*

THEO: Why am I not wearing a bra?
WALLACE: I was gonna make you that chocolate-coffee combo that you like, but I'm out of milk.
THEO: My outfit is exactly the same, yet my bra is gone. It's like a magic trick.
WALLACE: I'm out of juice too and I don't really trust the water. Maybe we should go for a walk and get some—
THEO: Wallace …
WALLACE: —pancakes!

ACT ONE

THEO: … stop playing house.

> *Beat.*

WALLACE: You were angry last night.

THEO: I'm not a bundle of ecstasy this morning either.

> *She picks her bra out from the twisted sheets.*

WALLACE: Couples get angry then there's wild sex and before you know it you're looking at—

THEO: There will be no wild sex!

WALLACE: —bedspreads together.

> *Beat.*

THEO: That's not why I came around last night.

> WALLACE *bows his head and returns to typing.*

Wallace? Wallace, come on. [*She sighs.*] I need your advice.

WALLACE: Okay, here's my advice: take off all your clothes and do those devilish things you do so well.

THEO: How can you be so articulate on the net and such a pathetic little pus rag in person?

WALLACE: I'm a troll, that's our thing. [*Deflating*] I don't know what you want here, Theo. You asked to move in with me and now here I am being the supportive partner.

THEO: It's a crapload more complicated than that now. Do the maths.

WALLACE: Maths? What maths?

THEO: We multiplied ourselves, Wallace!

> *Beat.*

WALLACE: Yeah, that might be a problem.

THEO: If we go through with this, we'll be dividing everything we *don't* have into smaller fractions. A fraction of zero over zero has no defined value, it's a mathematical impossibility …

WALLACE: Okay, I get that, but it's not like we're … Dickensian vagrants. We have some hope.

THEO: We cannot feed or clothe ourselves. [*Sighing*] That's why I'm trapped in *The Addams Family*.

WALLACE: Your folks are nothing like *The Addams Family*.

THEO: [*glaring*] The musical version.

WALLACE: Well, yes.
THEO: And you run a website for armchair hippies.
WALLACE: That's not fair.
THEO: Let's be serious, it's an outlet for people who are too lazy, apathetic, drug-fucked or plain old shit-scared to actually organise a proper protest about anything! Where's your revolution, Wallace?
WALLACE: It's a work in progress!

She snatches his laptop.

THEO: Do you know what I see here? Plump women in g-strings!
WALLACE: That's just a message from our sponsor.
THEO: But it's not a job, is it? Neither of us has a steady income. So, do the maths!
WALLACE: [*with a sigh*] It probably won't be that terrible.
THEO: Quantify, Wallace! Two plus one divided by a pittance equals sweet bugger all. We can't afford an extra stomach.
WALLACE: We can afford a small one.

He tries to kiss her. She ducks away from him.

Theo—

Her attention is focused on the laptop, as her mind kicks into gear.

THEO: Just … sit. Mummy's thinking.

Beat.

Shut your face. [*Hammering keys*] Find the debt-to-income ratio, debt over pre-tax income where income is known current monthly pre-tax assets … let's think now, um, known salary …?
WALLACE: Well, you've got the café gig … I make twelve grand at the comic shop, six at the grocer's, and the site pulls in … I dunno … about four hundred.
THEO: [*brightening*] A month!
WALLACE: Are you crazy?

THEO *frowns and violently punches in the numbers.*

This is big. [*To himself, solemnly*] New life. Birth. *Creatio ex nihilo.*
THEO: [*ignoring him*] Interest: using compound interest on best calculation as daily rate M equals P times one plus r over twelve times three hundred and sixty-five times t …

ACT ONE 39

WALLACE: [*brightening*] It's a major tick on my bucket list!
THEO: ... where r is the annual rate and t is the number of years ...
WALLACE: The universe is beautiful, Theo.
THEO: ... taking into account debt as monthly liabilities, so water, gas, electricity, food ...
WALLACE: [*with a cough*] Internet.
THEO: Plus, nappies, bottles, humidifiers, vaporisers, sterilisers, latches, cribs, tiny outfits, barrier creams ... [*Off his look*] They chafe!
WALLACE: Got it.
THEO: [*ramping up*] Then you've got baby monitors, baby tubs, baby mats, it's a whole refurb!
WALLACE: But ... fun, yeah?
THEO: Fuck no! What else? [*Counting on her fingers, rapid-fire*] Spoons, bibs, chairs, bowls ... [*back to typing, feverishly*] ... nursing bras, nursing pillows, nursing pads, breast pumps, nipple balm ...
WALLACE: Not every week, surely.

THEO *paces. Numbers float around her.*

THEO: [*triple time*] So, generating a 'child cost fixed rate payment formula' ... P equals A times r over twelve times one plus r over twelve to the power of twelve over one plus r over twelve to the power of twelve *minus* one, where P is monthly payments, A is the amount generated and r is the annual growth rate multiplied by the number of years old ... uh-huh, yep ...

She pauses to calculate, then resumes typing.

... then factoring in future liabilities ... let's see ... Baby Bounce, Playgroup, Kindergym, Little Kickers ...
WALLACE: [*pointing*] Who do you think you have in there ... David Beckham?
THEO: Then onto school fees, university fees, after-school sport, maybe an instrument, or a language ...
WALLACE: A language?!
THEO: ... wedding costs, housing deposit ...
WALLACE: Our kid is getting a house now?! Man, I hate this person!
THEO: And put that against projected outcome [*calculating*] ... frak! Current and projected debt-to-income ratio for the next twenty years is seventy-six point three seven per cent. We're numerically screwed.

Beat.

WALLACE: [*stunned*] I feel contaminated.

THEO: You and me both, Wallace.

She slams the laptop down. By now, she should be well out of breath.

Long beat.

WALLACE *heaves a sigh and tentatively approaches her.*

WALLACE: You've clearly thought this through. [*Coaxing a smile*] For what's it's worth—

THEO: I'm having anxiety dreams. Motherhood is like Russian roulette! I could give birth to a throwback. It could be eighty per cent Jasper.

WALLACE: [*grinning*] Or pure, undiluted Wallace.

THEO: Nature is so cruel.

He snatches his laptop back.

WALLACE: Jesus, Theo! Why can't you be optimistic for once? Why can't you just—

THEO: [*arms folded*] I'm a defensive pessimist—

WALLACE *jumps up and down.*

WALLACE: —let me finish a fucking sentence?!

Beat.

THEO: That was quite a tantrum.

WALLACE: Hang on … is this the sexy war? [*A light bulb moment.*] I've got a move for this!

He embraces her and goes in for the kiss.

THEO: Wallace!

She pushes him away. When he makes a second attempt, she twists his nipple.

WALLACE: Arrgh!

THEO: What are you doing?

WALLACE: [*rubbing his chest*] I'm … being … primal.

THEO: Primal?

He nods. She flicks him between the eyes.

ACT ONE

WALLACE *lets out an agonised cry.*

Someone thumps on the wall. Pomeranians howl.

Damn. [*Calling*] I'm sorry, Mr Barkass. We're having a sleepover.

A voice yells in a foreign language.

Yep ... yep, nah ... s'all good. Please stop beating the wall.

The thumping stops.

[*In a weak, embarrassed voice*] Thanks.

Long beat.

THEO *and* WALLACE *adopt forced whispers.*

I'm sorry.
WALLACE: Don't stress, he's mentally ill.
THEO: No, I mean ... I'm sorry I yelled at you and twisted your man-boob.
WALLACE: You mean my pec?
THEO: It's a full boob. [*More sincere*] Are you okay?
WALLACE: I'll recover. Sorry for being too manly.
THEO: You weren't. [*She grins.*] Sorry for calling you a pus rag.
WALLACE: I can be a bit of a pus rag sometimes. It's fine.
THEO: You're right, though. [*Shrugging*] I don't know what I want.
WALLACE: I'll tell you one thing ...

He gestures for her to follow him to the front door. They clear their throats and return to their normal voices.

Lights turn. Stars appear.

... you were *laissez-faire* about the breach in our condom. Very *laissez-faire*!
THEO: Wallace!
WALLACE: *Laissez-faire*!

She hits him playfully.

THEO: I didn't want this to happen.
WALLACE: But it's *not* the end of the world, is it? It's supposed to be a beginning. It could be, if we let it. [*With a smile*] You were very *laissez-faire*, Theo.
THEO: [*with a sigh*] Do you know why I go into bitch mode?

WALLACE: Because it's your first gear?

> *Beat.*
>
> *She thumps him again. He half-laughs, half-whimpers.*

THEO: Because I'm scared. [*She swallows.*] I'm terrified.

> *They draw close. A comet shoots overhead.*

I don't think I can be a mother.
WALLACE: I don't think I can be a real politician.
THEO: I'd vote for you.
WALLACE: I don't want you to vote for me. I want you by my side.
THEO: I can do both.
WALLACE: Maybe that's the point, Theo. Maybe we can do it all.
THEO: Hey, if you're having a career, I'm having one too!
WALLACE: And if you're having a baby, then so am I.

> *Beat.*

THEO: Shit.
WALLACE: What?
THEO: You're being cute.
WALLACE: [*with a grin*] Sorry.

> *She kisses him.*

THEO: It doesn't add up, Wallace.
WALLACE: I don't care.

> *Their foreheads touch.*

THEO: Whatever we decide, I have to tell Mum. [*Turning pale*] Oh God, I have to tell Dad!

> *Lights change, as* THEO *spins around.*

SCENE TWELVE

A spot appears on BABS. THEO *spins to face her.*

BABS: You *can't* tell him!
THEO: It's not like I have a choice.
BABS: He's not ready to be a grandfather. Do you know what that will do to his self-image? He nearly weeps every time he finds a new wrinkle.

ACT ONE

THEO: Sorry, I forgot this was all about his feelings.
BABS: Oh darling, that's not what I mean. I couldn't be happier for you.
THEO: Well, sure. [*Pointing*] You're, like, mega-maternal.
BABS: Thank you, dear.
THEO: You're like a walking cardigan. Or an ovum. [*She thinks.*] Or an ovum in a cardigan that just wants to hug everyone and make them try new kinds of exotic tea.
BABS: Have you experienced the Gingerbread Blast? Or the Herbal Rose Infusion?
THEO: Mum!
BABS: Sorry. I'm just a little squeamish. I wasn't even aware that you were romantically ... active.
THEO: *Mum!*
BABS: Sorry, sorry. [*She thinks.*] Well, I suppose we'll have to do a little bit of redecorating. I could turn my sewing room into a nursery. That might be nice. It catches a bit of a draft, but we could hang some drapes or paint penguins or something.
THEO: Yeah, I think Dad might get slightly suspicious at that point.
BABS: Ooh, I could knit booties!
THEO: If you like.
BABS: You never enjoyed my booties, Theodora. You used to lash out with those chubby little feet of yours and kick them off.
THEO: [*looking down*] They *are* chubby, aren't they? I've got duck feet. Hope my kid doesn't get those.
BABS: I used to find booties everywhere! Booties scattered all over the carpet, booties under the crib ... booties on the ceiling fan!
THEO: I apologise for failing to appreciate your booties. [*With a sigh*] What am I going to do, Mum?
BABS: You're going to make the best of it. The reverend will have things to say, of course. A baby born out of wedlock is a little on the nose.
THEO: Oh, for fu—
BABS: Theodora!
THEO: [*with a sigh*] Wedlock. Sounds just like a prison sentence.
BABS: [*drifting off*] Well, if the reverend refuses to baptise our new arrival, we'll just have to take our business elsewhere.
THEO: No one will be drowning my baby.
BABS: Perhaps a new congregation will be good for us.

THEO: You're not supposed to call him 'Reverend' anyhow. Learn his name.
BABS: [*dreamy*] I don't think my lemon slice gets nearly enough attention at the fête.
THEO: Mum, this isn't your baby. If I'm going to do this, I'm going to do it my way.
BABS: I detect a little judgement there.
THEO: It's not like that.
BABS: You were never easy, Theodora. Even in the womb, you were feistier than you should have been.
THEO: Again, I apologise. I should have been a more considerate foetus.
BABS: It was like a soccer match.
THEO: Must've been awful.
BABS: It's those fat calves of yours.
THEO: I get it, Mum.
BABS: Manly calves.
THEO: Cheers.

   Beat.

   THEO *opens her mouth to speak ...*

BABS: More like a soccer *riot*, actually. You know, when the Italian men get all huffy after the game and they start burning flags …?
THEO: [*groaning*] Mum, please ease up on the Catholic guilt.
BABS: Or are they Brazilian men? Some of them really are quite gorgeous.
THEO: Babs!
BABS: The point I'm making is that I suffered to bring you into this world, and sometimes … no, look at me … sometimes I think you forget that I'm a real flesh and blood person. I have feelings, Theodora. It would be nice if you put the kettle on for *me* every once in a while. In fact, it would be extra-nice if you would initiate a conversation instead of making me extract every single syllable. [*Downcast*] Just talk to me.
THEO: [*gently*] I *am* talking to you. It's hell.
BABS: Or just look at me with something other than boredom in your eyes.

   They stare daggers at each other.

THEO: Is this better?

ACT ONE

BABS: Pass me my knitting, I'm upset.
THEO: I thought we were having a conversation.
BABS: I'm upset and I want to stitch something!

> THEO *hands the knitting over.*

THEO: Do you think I should keep the baby?
BABS: …
THEO: [*prompting*] Well?
BABS: Oh, Theodora! Should that even be a question? It's not like it's a puppy you picked up from the shops. You can't just take it back because it wets everywhere.
THEO: I would never take a puppy back to the shops.
BABS: We'll find a gentle way to tell your father …
THEO: Who would take a puppy back to the shops? That's cruel!
BABS: … and then you can try your hand at motherhood.
THEO: Puppies are so trusting. [*Snapping back to reality*] But, do you really think Wallace and I can …?
BABS: Wallace? Is he the father?
THEO: Of course he's the father!
BABS: Little Wallace?
THEO: He's had a growth spurt!
BABS: But he's just a twig of a thing. You didn't hurt him, did you?
THEO: No!

> *Beat.*

Look, I never meant to disrespect your mothering technique.
BABS: It's not a 'technique', it's trial and error.
THEO: It's just that, with Dad, and … and … the band and the pills, and the police raids.
BABS: I thought you slept through the raids.
THEO: And the arguments.
BABS: [*drifting off again*] The police broke my china hutch.
THEO: And the fires.
BABS: That sergeant could dance though, I'll give him that.
THEO: [*shuddering*] And those weird toga parties.
BABS: [*with a dismissive wave*] We only had half a dozen of those.
THEO: And the guy … remember the guy?
BABS: What guy?

THEO: The beardy guy who lived in our hammock.
BABS: [*remembering*] Shred Lord!
THEO: See? It hasn't exactly been a textbook upbringing!
BABS: He never ate enough. I could always see his ribs.
THEO: So, please don't take any of this as a criticism …

    BABS *deflates.*

BABS: Other children loved to visit. Truthfully, I think some of them were jealous. Your father was always such fun.
THEO: I have the dubious honour of being the only human being you two have raised. [*She swallows.*] If I'm being open, there are some pitfalls … or, hurdles … let's say hurdles … I'd like to avoid.
BABS: Hurdles? Hmph.

    She puts her knitting down.

I have always strived to offer you balance, Theodora. I took you to Sunday School.
THEO: Yeah, those freaks actually made me feel semi-normal.
BABS: You shouldn't use harsh words to describe children.
THEO: I wasn't describing the children.
BABS: [*snapping her fingers*] I know what else I did … I encouraged you to study business. Your father wanted you to take a year off, but I intervened. I said 'Jasper, if she wants to be a dull accountant, let her be a dull accountant.'
THEO: Great. Real supportive.
BABS: Oh, he made such a fuss.
THEO: [*caustically*] How unexpected.
BABS: It started a terrible row.
THEO: Do you know what stuns me? The fact that you two got together in the first place … chalk and cheese actually went out on a date.
BABS: Am I chalk or am I cheese?
THEO: He's definitely cheese.
BABS: We were different people back then, Theodora. That's what I'm trying to tell you. Couples grow. They find their … well, their natural rhythm.
THEO: And do you have any regrets?
BABS: Not one.
THEO: Are you sure? I mean, if I hadn't come along …

BABS: [*with a smile*] But you did.

> *Purple spots suddenly illuminate the stage.*
>
> *Music kicks in.*
>
> JASPER *appears upstage right, a silhouette in crisscrossing purple beams. Smoke rises. Music video wind runs through his hair. We're back in fantasy land. He wears double denim and sports an 80s mullet and impressive power moustache.*
>
> *Seductively,* JASPER *sings. It's a clichéd karaoke number—'Bette Davis Eyes' or similar—but he makes it work.*
>
> *He snakes downstage, approaching the audience, swaying in time with the beat.*
>
> ANNI *appears upstage left, golden hair slicked down, cheeks caked in glitter. She wears a tux with gingham lining and matching velvet gloves. Somewhere between Kim Carnes, Blondie and—her namesake—Annie Lennox. She sings with* JASPER, *her sultry tones echoing around the auditorium.*
>
> *In their second verse, a spotlight lands on* BABS, *in pigtails, wearing a Catholic school uniform. She watches* JASPER *and runs her fingers nervously over her crucifix as he gyrates.*
>
> *He holds out his hand to her, pitching the lyrics her way.*
>
> *She looks over her shoulder and then realises he's singing to her.*
>
> *Beat.*
>
> *She points a finger at herself. ('Who, me?')*
>
> *He nods. ('Yes, you!')*
>
> *The rest of the cast appears in silhouette, pounding the stage to the beat.*
>
> JASPER *and* BABS *approach each other and begin to dance.*
>
> *Smoke swirls, lights flash and the song carries them away ...*

END OF ACT ONE

ACT TWO: GLORIOUS

SCENE ONE

Darkness. Keys pound a typewriter.

ANNI: [*voiceover*] Once upon a time, there lived a king and queen who wished for a child. But, for the longest time, they had none.

Lights slowly rise.

ANNI sits stage right, hunched over an antique typewriter. She looks the part: thick-rimmed glasses, pencil skirt and—naturally—a gingham blouse. Her words appear as typed letters or calligraphy, projected all around.

One morning, as the queen was bathing in a spring and dreaming of a child, an old mother frog leapt up, up, out of the water and said to her …

Spotlight on the MAGIC FROG.

MAGIC FROG: Thy wish be granted, majesty. Before the great bauble hath turned, a princess shalt be birthed into thine house.

ANNI: Now, everyone knows that frogs are magical creatures and only the thickest fools doubt them at their word. So, precisely nine and a half months later, the queen had a very, very bad day.

Spotlight on QUEEN BARBARELLA *in full medieval dress, crying out. She's in labour and hating it as much as most people do.*

QUEEN BARBARELLA: *Arrrgggh!*

MAGIC FROG: Just one more push, majesty.

MAGIC FROG dons a surgical mask and gloves. She carries forceps in her webbed hands.

QUEEN BARBARELLA: *Art thou qualified?!*

MAGIC FROG: Not in the slightest, my queen.

They freeze.

ANNI: It didn't take long for word to spread throughout the land. Every lord and lady, every peasant, every serf and every scribe came to pay homage to the newborn princess.

Spotlight on TOWN CRIER *in pantaloons. He waves his bell and reads from a scroll that reaches all the way down to the floor.*

TOWN CRIER: Hear ye, hear ye! Queen Barbarella hath dropped her bundle! All hail the new princess!

ALL: Hail! Hail!

He freezes.

ANNI: Of course, one cannot expect a princess to be meek. It wasn't long before the lucky child began to question her elders … and wrapped within those questions there were judgements. The king was *not* amused.

Spotlight on KING OF SWING. *Vintage Memphis jumpsuit. Flashy tassels. Studded boots.*

KING OF SWING: The accursed daughter disrespects me. Before she dropped out of mine bride, I was the ruler of all. I was loved—nay—adored!

MAGIC FROG *hops over to him.*

MAGIC FROG: The princess will earn her own crown in time.

KING OF SWING: She will do no such thing!

MAGIC FROG: 'Tis the way of the worlds, my liege. When thy child's star rises, thou must be prepared to stand aside.

KING OF SWING: Stand aside? What tosh! What scandal! To the locker with this amphibian! Off with her impudent head!

QUEEN BARBARELLA: How now, my king?

She curtsies.

Wouldst thou deny thine own daughter?

Beat.

KING OF SWING: Yes.

They freeze.

ANNI: The pleas of noble Queen Barbarella did nothing to cool her husband's sizzling blood. Her words were wasted. The king would not be usurped, would not be forgotten, not even to make way for his own—

ACT TWO

THEO *enters, now visibly pregnant.*

THEO: What are you doing?

ANNI's *fingers hover over the typewriter keys. Busted.*

ANNI: [*with forced cheer*] Literature, Theo! The most refined form of artistic expression! The question minus the answer!

THEO: Get a job.

ANNI: Oh, come on … I'm telling your story.

THEO: It's not yours to tell.

ANNI: Then tell it with me!

She guides THEO *over to the typewriter.*

I was just about to introduce the villain.

ANNI *cracks her knuckles and returns to the keys.*

The king sent for his faithful emissary, the carrier pigeon, but little did he know a liar bird had taken her place. [*To* THEO] That's liar with an 'i' and an 'a', get it?

LIAR BIRD *enters, smoking a tiny cigarette.*

KING OF SWING: Come hither, little pigeon. I have an errand for thee!

LIAR BIRD: I know what thou seekest, noble king … a means of taming thine spirited child.

ANNI: So the liar bird took to the heavens, knowing the king would follow. Over the glade she flew, and beyond the marsh. The king kept pace on horseback, never suspecting that their destination was anything *but* heavenly …

Spotlight on APOTHECARY, *cloaked and hunched.*

APOTHECARY: Sign mine parchment, natty king.

KING OF SWING: Wife, fetch me a quill!

APOTHECARY: Surrender thy soul and I shall make thou immortal!

THEO: Stop it!

They freeze. Lights fade on the little pantomime.

ANNI *deflates.*

ANNI: Where's your sense of whimsy?

THEO: This is absurd.

ANNI: No, it's magical realism. [*Excited*] Oooh, are we having an artistic debate, Theo?

THEO: You're turning my life into a joke.
ANNI: Into art!

> THEO *tears at her hair.*

THEO: Fuck art!
ANNI: You don't mean that.
THEO: Yes, I do! Religion used to be the opiate of the masses, but now we have art. It's the emperor's new clothes, only not as funny.
ANNI: Art brings people together.
THEO: That's a lie! It rips them to shreds! [*Calmer*] Believe me, I know. I'm sick of it all.

> *She walks away from the typewriter, dropping pages as she goes.*

'Meaning'. 'Substance'. A 'message' behind everything. [*With a bitter laugh*] Do you know what it all adds up to? Vacant platitudes for the dumb, the lucky, the under-worked and the self-involved. Real life isn't neat. Real life can't be packaged.

> ANNI *claps her hands.*

ANNI: Bravo! What an act!
THEO: I don't have an act!
ANNI: You're as desperate for approval as everyone else, Theo. Being ordinary—that's your act!
THEO: I want you out of my head.
ANNI: Truly? I'm not sure your head agrees with you.

> THEO *steps towards* ANNI *and immediately doubles over, nauseous. White strobe lights flicker and die.*

THEO: Go away—

> *She cups her hands over her mouth.*

BABS: [*offstage*] Theodora!

> BABS *enters. She hurries to* THEO, *carrying a bucket.*

Easy, pet. Morning sickness is perfectly normal.
THEO: At three p.m.?
BABS: Well, it's more of a guideline really. In fact, the reverend says—
THEO: Oh, like he's an expert on childbirth.

> *She dips her head in the bucket.*
>
> *Beat.*

ACT TWO

She emerges.

You still don't know his name, do you?

BABS: [*deflating*] No, I don't … what am I supposed to call him? Cardinal? Padre? 'Holy Father' just sounds creepy.

THEO: It's Catholicism! Creepy is all they have left!

THEO returns to the bucket. BABS rubs her back.

BABS: There, there. It'll pass in a moment.

ANNI grins her gremlin grin and vanishes.

THEO: [*exhaling*] I'm okay.

She pushes the bucket to one side.

Boy, pregnancy is a mindfuck.

BABS: Wait until you have a teenager in the kitchen.

THEO: I used to cook!

Beat.

Has Dad come home yet?

BABS pats her hand.

BABS: He won't be long. [*Warmly*] Oh, darling, I only wish I could prepare you for family life.

She sighs.

Passionless nights in watching *Doctor Who*. Fruitless arguments about hoovering or toilet roll holders, or if a new week begins on Sunday or Monday.

THEO: Monday, clearly.

BABS: [*annoyed*] Sunday.

THEO: Wallace and I will have our own arguments.

BABS: Yes, I'm sure.

THEO: And we haven't decided anything, remember. This might not be the fairytale you expect. [*Off her look*] Real life is messy.

It takes a second for BABS to accept this. She nods and turns to leave.

BABS: You're alright aren't you, Theodora? Only sometimes your eyes glaze over and your mouth twitches, and I really don't know where you drift off to.

THEO: I'm here, Babs.

> BABS *isn't certain.*

BABS: [*warily*] Don't fret about your father. He's just off finding himself.
THEO: [*groaning*] Again?
BABS: He keeps getting lost.

> *She goes.*

> THEO *glances back at the typewriter … it's still lit, stage right.*

THEO: [*to herself*] For once I know the feeling.

> *An Indian gong punctuates her words.*

> *A spotlight appears on* JASPER.

SCENE TWO

JASPER *sits on a large cushion, cross-legged, surrounded by incense. He's wearing a dhoti* (*Indian skirt*) *and colourful turban. Grating, generic, not-quite-Indian muzak plays.*

CHAD'*s voice guides the meditation.*

CHAD: [*voiceover*] Breathe. [*A long inhalation.*] Breathe deep. [*He exhales.*] Let your cares wash down the Ganges. Today's session is all about you. Not the 'you' you think you know, but the 'you' you haven't met yet. The new you. The *true* you.
JASPER: Sounds like *The Cat in the Hat*.
CHAD: [*voiceover*] Silence your mind. Embrace thoughtlessness. [*A longer inhalation.*] Turn to side B.
JASPER: Huh? Aw, not again.

> *The muzak cuts off abruptly.* JASPER *leaves his cushion and fumbles around with the tape recorder.*

I was just starting to feel thoughtless.

> *His phone rings.*

[*Picking up*] Hello?

> *A spotlight illuminates* CHAD, *with not a care in the world. He's wearing his robe and sipping a martini.*

CHAD: How's my favourite protégé?

ACT TWO

JASPER: I've just been listening to your tapes, Mr Mombardo. Why don't you release a CD? Or a digital download?
CHAD: [*smirking*] Digital download. What have I told you about earthly possessions? Besides, tapes are more personal. Play it over the phone.
JASPER: Are you serious?
CHAD: Go on, play it.

> JASPER *turns the tape around and presses 'play'. The muzak returns.*

Love this track. I've got a guy. Pakistani guy. He nails the dreamy stuff, don't you reckon?
JASPER: Yeah, it's … um … evocative.
CHAD: Ssh, I'm about to say something.

> *He presses his head tight to the earpiece, hanging on his own words.*

[*Voiceover*] To find your true self, you need more than a mirror. You need open eyes, open heart and open soul.

> JASPER *pauses the tape.*

JASPER: Listen, Mr Mombardo …
CHAD: I *am* listening. I am, and always have been, in love with the melodious sound of my own wisdom repeated back to me.

> CHAD *might be joking, it's hard to tell … but* JASPER *laughs awkwardly all the same.*

[*Peevish*] Open soul, Jasper. Remember that. Eyes are useless if your soul is closed.
JASPER: I appreciate your insight, but—
CHAD: Your eyes can deceive you … don't trust them.
JASPER: Did you just quote from *Star Wars?*
CHAD: No, that one is mine.
JASPER: I'm pretty sure Kenobi got there first.
CHAD: Earthly possessions, Jasper. They must be discarded.
JASPER: I'll get around to that.
CHAD: You must unlearn what you have learned.
JASPER: Now, honestly—
CHAD: I'm calling because your card is dead.
JASPER: Pardon?

CHAD: Dead as in empty, tapped out.
JASPER: Oh. Sorry. Look, maybe it's best that I don't spend anymore—
CHAD: [*slapping his head*] And then there's the other thing!
JASPER: Other thing?
CHAD: I almost forgot! I can be a real butter brain. My contact left me a message. You know, my Sony contact?
JASPER: I don't … Sony, are you serious?
CHAD: [*with a grin*] For realsies! I haven't mentioned her?
JASPER: No.
CHAD: Wow, I'm such a ditz. Anyways, if we get this card thing sorted, maybe we can organise a lunch …?

> *Beat.*
>
> JASPER *deliberates silently with himself.*

JASPER: How about dinner? My wife and I would love to have you around to our place.
CHAD: Oh, Jasper … I wouldn't want to be any trouble. Shall we say eight o'clock?
JASPER: It's no trouble, Mr Mombardo.
CHAD: Call me Chad.

> *Lights fade.*

SCENE THREE

Spotlight on WALLACE. *He's typing, as always, and sucking ice coffee through a straw.*

WALLACE: [*to himself, sing-song*] I'm so busy, I'm so busy, I'm so busy, I'm so horny, I'm so busy, I'm so busy.

> *There is a knock at the door.*

[*Hopeful*] Hey, babe!
FIGSBY: [*offstage*] I'm not your babe.
WALLACE: Come in.

> FIGSBY *enters, dragging a cardboard box. She's dressed like an armchair revolutionary—expensive grunge.*

FIGSBY: Where do you want this stuff?
WALLACE: Right there is fine. Thanks for helping us out.

ACT TWO

They tear the box open together.

FIGSBY: So, who is the girl? Wait, I don't want to know.
WALLACE: I wasn't going to tell you.
FIGSBY: [*horrified*] Tell me!
WALLACE: You just said you didn't want to know.
FIGSBY: Yes, but I thought you would argue. You *have* to tell me! Tell me everything! Maybe draw a picture.
WALLACE: I'm not going to draw you a picture of how I conceived my child.
FIGSBY: I would draw one for you.
WALLACE: And I would feel really uncomfortable looking at it.

> WALLACE *digs into the box and withdraws a pink and white carton.*

[*Reading*] 'The Silly Stork Home Pregnancy Test'. [*He grins.*] Nice work, Figsby.
FIGSBY: There are twelve of those in there.
WALLACE: Twelve?
FIGSBY: We have to be sure.
WALLACE: I don't think she can pee that much.

> FIGSBY *nods and sticks her hand in the box. She withdraws two large water bottles.*

FIGSBY: Ta-da! I thought of everything. I'm your number one gal!
WALLACE: I'm still not gonna tell you who she is.
FIGSBY: Alright, I'll tell you something first. Nobody is aware of this. [*Proudly*] I slept with every woman in my tango class.

> WALLACE *is shocked.*

What?
WALLACE: I didn't know you could dance.
FIGSBY: Singer, dancer, lover … I'm a triple threat!
WALLACE: Could you teach me?

> *She looks him up and down.*

FIGSBY: Do you have any sense of rhythm?
WALLACE: I can waltz!
FIGSBY: Old people can waltz, Wallace.

WALLACE *shrugs.*

Dead people can waltz. [*Grinning*] Come on, who is she?

WALLACE: How much do I owe you?

FIGSBY: Just give me a name!

WALLACE: [*giving in*] Somebody wise, somebody funny. Somebody who stands for something. Do you know how long I have been itching for that?

Beat.

FIGSBY*'s grin broadens.*

FIGSBY: Ooooh, you sound so into her. [*Confused*] Is it a 'her'? It's okay, I won't judge.

WALLACE: Why would I need twelve home pregnancy kits if I was dating a dude?

FIGSBY: [*gently*] I've been expecting you to follow me out of the closet any day now.

WALLACE: Figsby, you're sassy, you're brilliant, but I'm keeping this part of my life under wraps. Think of me as one of those more uptight, conventional revolutionary warriors.

FIGSBY: [*pouting*] I'm your wingman and you've clipped me!

WALLACE: You can't be my wingman.

FIGSBY: Wallace, my grandma has bigger balls than you.

WALLACE: I'm trying to be cool!

FIGSBY: You'll *never* be cool!

They turn away from each other. Both are a bit pissy.

WALLACE: Alright, I get it, I'm sorry for keeping my cards so close to my chest. It's just an awkward time.

FIGSBY: Meanwhile … the revolution is going down the U-bend.

WALLACE: S-bend.

FIGSBY: What?

WALLACE: You're talking about a dunny, right?

FIGSBY: I don't know.

WALLACE: Leave it with me, I'll inspire the troops.

FIGSBY: Do I look like a fucking plumber?

WALLACE: I'll sort it all out, Figsby. Just let me put some quality hours into my personal life first.

ACT TWO 59

FIGSBY: We're not even fighting Abbott anymore. The old rules have changed. Half of your supporters have left.
WALLACE: I have seven supporters.
FIGSBY: So?
WALLACE: So how could half of them have left?
FIGSBY: [*urgently*] They don't believe!
WALLACE: Three point five guys have walked out, is that what you're telling me?
FIGSBY: Three guys and ... [*She mumbles.*]
WALLACE: Who?

> *Beat.*

FIGSBY: My grandma.

> *This news hits hard.* WALLACE *is devastated.*

WALLACE: Damn. [*Hurt*] Really?
FIGSBY: I know, it's awful ... she has been the key to the whole operation!

> SASHA *barges in. Her look is even grungier than* FIGSBY*'s and, like her sister in arms, she has spent serious money to make it work. Vivid hair. Evil panda eyes. Careful tears in all her layers.*

SASHA: This is a crisis meeting!
WALLACE: [*with sarcasm*] Oh no, please, do come in, Sash. [*He rolls his eyes.*] Why knock?

> *She pulls a lollipop from her mouth and whacks* WALLACE *with it.*

SASHA: We need your head in the game, mate! Abbott is history! The pope's bitch tapped out in the second round!
FIGSBY: *All bets are off!*

> WALLACE *sighs with pleasure. His lips spread into a hearty grin.*

WALLACE: You're right ... we got him, girls. Those leaflets really made all the difference.
SASHA: You can masturbate about it later, that's not why I'm here. Figsby says you're losing your edge.
WALLACE: No, I'm still edgy. Prickly even.
FIGSBY: [*to* SASHA] He's in love.
SASHA: Fuuuucck ... we do *not* have time for that!
WALLACE: There's always time for that!

SASHA *gives him another beating with her lollipop.*

SASHA: You begged us to be at the top of the ticket, remember? You cried into your Weet-Bix! We didn't have to be nice to you then, did we?

FIGSBY: [*sheepishly*] I voted for Sash.

WALLACE: And I vetoed that motion because Sash is the Princess of Hell!

FIGSBY: Why do *you* get a veto?

SASHA: We *all* get a veto, that's why nothing gets done!

Stalemate.

Tempers cool.

When they next speak, their tones are much calmer, if a little icy.

WALLACE: I promised I would come through for my comrades. That was a hardcore campaign promise. But, even so—

SASHA: You wailed for this job.

WALLACE: Yes, I wailed.

FIGSBY: And we caved.

WALLACE: Thank you both, it was very compassionate.

SASHA: So now you have to dance, my little meat puppet. This isn't about *your* feelings.

WALLACE: I hear you.

FIGSBY: Do you though?

WALLACE: I do.

SASHA: You'd better! 'Cos Abbott was just the appetiser … you know who's coming for your compact little arse now, don't you? The man with the silver tongue!

WALLACE: [*appalled*] Jesus.

SASHA: Turnbull is some next level shit!

WALLACE: Well, to be fair, we don't know what he'll be like.

SASHA: A lot like the rest of the neocons—

FIGSBY: —but sexier!

WALLACE tries to steer the conversation back on course.

WALLACE: Look, I know you're just trying to grate my cheese, and I used to get worked up about all of this, but I'm not actually certain where my head should be anymore.

SASHA: Are you totally wussing out on us, Wallace?

WALLACE: My priorities are in a state of adjustment.

ACT TWO 61

He braces for the explosion ...

SASHA: [*cold fury*] Open your ears wide, you little wiener yanker, there's no backing out of this.

WALLACE: I—I—I never said—

SASHA: We need you to raise your voice!

FIGSBY: *Fight the power!*

WALLACE: Yeah, no, I will. I'll—I'll fight the power, but the thing is ... [*to* SASHA] please don't hurt me ... the thing ... the crucial thing is that Theo comes first.

FIGSBY: Ha! Theo! *That's* her name!

WALLACE: [*with a sigh*] That's her name.

FIGSBY: Are you *sure* she's not a dude?

WALLACE: She's not a dude.

FIGSBY: And you feel all sorts of tingly feelings when you think about her?

WALLACE: ...

FIGSBY raises her eyebrows at SASHA, who is taken aback.

SASHA: Must be some woman.

WALLACE: [*non-committal*] Must be.

They advance on WALLACE.

SASHA: But is she enough to make you abandon your revolutionary brothers and sisters?

FIGSBY: And your principles?

SASHA: And your country?

WALLACE: Enough to make me pause.

FIGSBY's grin returns.

FIGSBY: Sounds like the real thing!

SASHA: [*unimpressed*] Well, fuck a palomino.

WALLACE: Nobody meant for this to happen, but it feels right.

SASHA: I always said he was flaccid.

FIGSBY: You gonna man up and ask her to marry you?

WALLACE considers this carefully. He breaks into a massive grin of his own.

WALLACE: You bet her sweet tuchus I will.

Frenzied breathing builds. Lights change.

SCENE FOUR

THEO *sits, legs spread, with her hands on her belly. She is puffing like a train while* BABS *crouches behind her and reads from an old Lamaze book. An animated birth may be projected around them.*

BABS: Put two fingers together and place them on your belly. Just the two, Theodora. Now, take a big inhale, relaxing your abdominals … shoulders still … spine straight … now exhale and contract. Contract, Theodora.
THEO: I'm going to pass out.
BABS: Well, the girl in the cartoon is doing much better than you are, my love. She has flawless posture.
THEO: It's not a competition.
BABS: Look at her stance. She could do ballet.

A knock on the door.

THEO: Dammit!

BABS *helps* THEO *to her feet and throws a robe over her.* THEO *quickly ties it up and covers her belly.*

BABS: [*calling*] It's open.

WALLACE *rushes in, words flying from his mouth.*

WALLACE: Right, I know you said you needed space, and I've backed off obediently, but I want *you* to know that I've been doing a great deal of soul-searching and we really do need to think.
THEO: Think?
WALLACE: Yes, think about the road ahead!
THEO: Wallace, anything you can think of, I've generally thought of first.
WALLACE: But if you really are pregnant—
THEO / BABS: [*together, stunned*] If?
WALLACE: —we need to work out a strategy, a line of attack!
THEO: It's not a campaign launch, you goober.
WALLACE: I'm well-aware of the difference, thank you, but the principle—
THEO: You can't solve it with a citizen's jury.

BABS *clears her throat.*

BABS: Would anyone like an Iced VoVo?

ACT TWO

WALLACE: Oh, hey Babs! [*Scared*] Mrs Sprout.

He stares at her, horrified.

[*In a stage whisper*] She knows, doesn't she?
BABS: You must be feeling awfully proud of yourself, Wallace Bobbottom.
WALLACE: I'm a little contrite.
BABS: Whatever did Pam and Terry say?
WALLACE: Nothing yet. [*Squirming*] I texted them, but …
THEO: Wallace!
BABS: [*tutting*] And you were supposed to be their *good* son.
THEO: Give us a moment?

BABS sighs and turns to go.

BABS: He hasn't grown any more impressive. Must be one of those cheese and chive things you keep mentioning.
THEO: Chalk and cheese.
WALLACE: We're not chalk and cheese! [*Peevishly*] We're peanut butter and jelly.

They wait for BABS to go.

I wish you wouldn't shut me out, Theo. This could still be a fairytale.
THEO: Defensive pessimism: plan for the worst, hope for the best.
ANNI: Or you could just jump and hope there's a net! That's what I do!

ANNI appears, in a projection.

THEO: [*to ANNI*] Go away!
WALLACE: Fine. I'll go.
THEO: I wasn't talking to—
WALLACE: Sooner or later, we'll have to come to some arrangement.

He moves downstage, his back to THEO. A wedding ring glints from between his fingers. THEO doesn't see it.

I'll come back tonight when you've had a chance to simmer down.
THEO: Wallace—

But he's already out the door.

Shit!
ANNI: Oh, cry me a river, Theo. You're so grouchy with the world.
THEO: I hate you.

ANNI: And so blinkered. While you're proclaiming your right to be inconsequential, the people you love are striving. Little Wallace wants to change the course of political history, and as for your poor father … well, he never gives up.

THEO: You're not real, Anni. You're just the idea of a person.

> ANNI *steps out of the projection, into the flesh. For the first time she is dressed identically to* THEO.

ANNI: Maybe you're right.

> *The two stare at each other.*

But you need me, Theo. I make you interesting.

THEO: We'll see.

ANNI: Oh yes, it won't be long now, and we'll definitely see.

> *She looks down at* THEO*'s belly.*

They say each new generation is an improvement on the one before. [*Smiling*] Have you thought of a name yet?

> THEO *isn't listening.*

THEO: Get out of my head.

> *She marches away, leaving* ANNI *alone.*

ANNI: I'm not in your head, sweetie.

> *Thunder rumbles.*

> *A spotlight appears on* WALLACE, *caught in the storm, fumbling with his big, black umbrella.*

> ANNI *opens a little gingham umbrella and joins him.*

She'll come around.

WALLACE: Pardon?

ANNI: Whoever you've been crying over. She'll come around, we always do.

WALLACE: I'm not crying, it's just … [*He sighs.*] Do you have a …?

> *She hands him her handkerchief.*

Thanks.

> *He wipe his eyes.*

ANNI: I love nights like this.

ACT TWO 65

WALLACE: Storms? [*Smiling*] Me too.
ANNI: It feels like something building … something big is about to happen.

She looks at him, a shy smile.

Something extraordinary.

Beat.

WALLACE: Y'think?
ANNI: [*frowning*] Don't you?
WALLACE: I don't know if I believe in the extraordinary anymore.
ANNI: Oh, it's all extraordinary.

They look up at the sky.

I think thunder may be my favourite sound.

WALLACE *offers her the handkerchief.*

You can give it back to me one day.

He nods and turns to leave.

Beat.

He turns back.

WALLACE: An orchestra tuning. Right before the show begins. That's my favourite sound.

ANNI *closes her eyes.*

ANNI: I remember.
WALLACE: [*unnerved*] What's your name?
ANNI: Anni.
WALLACE: [*smiling*] Like the orphan.
ANNI: I hope not.

Beat.

WALLACE: Don't stay out in the cold, Anni.

He goes, leaving ANNI *crying softly in the rain.*
As the lights change, hysterical laughter builds.

SCENE FIVE

Lights rise. THEO *and* BABS *are sharing a pot of tea.* THEO *jiggles a plate in front of her mother. Both are laughing hard.*

THEO: Have another cookie. [*With a huge smile*] They're awesome!
BABS: You're not trying to make me put on weight, are you, dear?
THEO: No, I'm trying to make you high.

> *Beat.*
>
> BABS *bursts into a fresh explosion of laughter. It is clear that something is—very—wrong with the cookies.*

You were talking about your first boyfriend.
BABS: It's a short story. [*Laughing*] Short and limp!

> *She suddenly becomes serious, even grave.*

He couldn't get it up. Erectile Malfunction.

> THEO *matches her mother's solemn tone.*

THEO: Were you sympathetic?
BABS: No, dear … I was young and frisky. I didn't have that kind of time.
THEO: What did you say?
BABS: I told him I wanted a penis. A functional penis. Like it says on the label.
THEO: His penis had a label?
BABS: I don't suppose it was a very kind response.
THEO: You should write to him.
BABS: Should I?
THEO: You should write to him and apologise, say 'it's not you, it's me'.
BABS: But it's him. It's his penis.
THEO: [*nodding*] It's his penis, but you could be supportive.
BABS: I supported it. With my pinkie finger. Nothing.
THEO: You need to make it right. Tell him there's no hard feelings.

> *Beat.*
>
> *They burst out laughing once again.*

Was he the only one? [*Prompting*] Before Dad?

ACT TWO 67

BABS: Oh, there's only been one, really. Compared to your father, other boys just seemed ... tedious. But then I believe there *should* only be one. I guess I'm old and set in my ways.

THEO: Better than being young and insecure.

BABS: Oh, don't be silly. You're a lioness.

THEO: I'm completely out of my depth. People shouldn't be able to create new life until they're at least seventy-eight. You weren't ready. I'm not even close to ready.

BABS: Nobody is ever ready. That's why most of the time it's an accident.

THEO rises from the table, rubbing her belly.

THEO: I don't even know what kind of bun I have in my little ... microwave. Can you imagine Theo 2.0? Or what if it's like Dad? Another Jasper?

BABS: Is that what you're afraid of?

THEO: I said it to Wallace and he brushed it off like it didn't mean anything, but it's a legitimate concern!

She takes a bite of a cookie, speaking through scattering crumbs.

Wallace is *not* sexy. That boy is so thin and yet sooo plump at the same time it's ... really, it's mythic. When he gets naked, you can see his ribs *and* his beer gut. He's like the Frankenstein of ugly dudes.

BABS: Yes, I imagine that's accurate.

THEO: [*ignoring her*] Strictly speaking, the likelihood of my child being *exactly* like Wallace or Dad is one in two, but if I factor in the variables of narcissism, baldness, anaemia, stupidity, body odour, conspicuous ribs ... hmm, outcomes: let's say six ... events: one, being born ... so one divided by six, one sixth, point one six six six ...

The figures appear around her: '1/6, .1666, 16.6%'.

Sixteen point six per cent. Not bad ... but this is simplistic! The baby could have multiple random variables, seen as independent events, so if I calculate these as separate probabilities ...

BABS *sips her tea as* THEO *grabs her napkin and writes furiously, muttering under her breath.*

... comes to zero point six nine four three. Seriously? A sixty-nine point four three per cent likelihood of a stinky, bald, narcissistic, dumbass Wallace? That's just not fair.

BABS: [*smiling*] But, on the cheerier side, it could be rather like me!
THEO: Oh, shit!
BABS: Language!

    THEO *exhales. Her eyes shift back down to her belly.*

THEO: Sometimes I worry that I won't be good enough for this, and then … other times … it sounds bad, but … I wonder if I'm not too good.
BABS: Too good?
THEO: Women fought to be more than mothers. They marched in the streets for the right to be … something other than a baby factory. I feel like I'm betraying them.
BABS: You want more?
THEO: Hell yeah I want more!
BABS: My dear, you and your father are much more alike than either of you will ever admit.
THEO: I'm gonna pretend that's the cookie talking.

    BABS *pours them both a fresh cup of tea.*

BABS: The trap you're falling into is thinking that motherhood cannot possibly be an empowering choice.
THEO: But can it be?
BABS: It absolutely can. It's a *choice*.
THEO: Well, for you …
BABS: [*with a sigh*] Motherhood doesn't have to define you, Theodora. It's not some great, gloomy shadow hanging over your entire existence. Frankly, it's just a hobby.
THEO: Wait, no … hang on a minute … no, no … you're supposed to be maternal! Mega-maternal! We agreed!
BABS: It comes and goes. I mean, I know you want to move out. You haven't exactly been gracious about it these past few days … and I haven't done anything to stop you, have I?
THEO: [*gasping*] Oh, my royal shit! Who are you?
BABS: It's like skiing.
THEO: Skiing?
BABS: Motherhood is something a woman *may* choose to do if and when the opportunity presents itself. [*She snaps her fingers.*] Fruit picking, there's another one.

ACT TWO

THEO: I ... I—I ... this is ... wrong.

> THEO *slumps back into her chair.* BABS *passes a cup across the table.*

BABS: I'll have you know, Little Miss Cranky ... I have been a *lot* of other things besides a full-time mummy. I ran my own shop. I backpacked through the Congo.

> *She takes a sip.*

For a few months in the early nineties I was a nude dancer.

> THEO *spits tea all over herself.*

That's right. I'll give you my stage name and you can run it through the Google.

THEO: *No!*

BABS: Come on, I'll whisper it.

THEO: You were a stripper? Mum, you're a Catholic!

BABS: There was no stripping.

THEO: [*relieved*] Thank goodness.

BABS: No, no, I started naked and then I ... well, I sort've stayed naked. With some high kicks. And a sashay.

THEO: You're a Catholic who bakes for the church.

BABS: There were disco lights so it was all very tasteful.

THEO: You're a Catholic who makes even the reverend feel guilty.

BABS: I can still do the robot. Look—

> *She does.*

THEO: *You're my mum!*

> *Beat.*

BABS: [*with a knowing smile*] Sometimes.

THEO: [*with a sigh*] Sometimes.

> BABS *pats* THEO *on the knee.*

BABS: I don't think you should have any more cookies, dear. They don't agree with you.

> *She turns to go.*

THEO: I'm scared.

> *Beat.*

BABS: Do you know what? You'll be a wonderful mother.
THEO: I won't.
BABS: You'll be terrifying and courageous, and clever, and kind.

>   *Long beat.*

THEO: I like you.
BABS: You like me?
THEO: Well, I *have* to love you … that's a contract written in blood, but … but, I like you.

>   BABS *squeezes her hand.*

BABS: I like you too.
THEO: Now don't cry.
BABS: No, no I wouldn't dream of it. [*Excited*] Ooh, I have another man story! This is a *milkman* story! When I was seventeen—

>   JASPER *bursts in, loving life.*

JASPER: Babs, we have a dinner guest!
BABS: A guest? But I was only going to make fish fingers.
JASPER: That won't cut it. We need to dig out the good silverware. There's a very important man coming over.
THEO: Let me guess … an Aztec witchdoctor?
JASPER: Oh, so witty.

>   *He ruffles her hair. She slaps him away.*

THEO: A shaman? A monk?
JASPER: Don't be smart, Theo.
THEO: Hmm. You're putting on your adult voice. It must be someone pretty mystical.
JASPER: Just a friend.

>   *He kisses* BABS *on the cheek.*

You don't mind, do you? Put me to work: I'll slice, I'll dice … whatever it takes.
BABS: [*to* THEO] I think we should tell him. Go on, let's be devils.
THEO: What? No, you said he couldn't handle it.
BABS: Bullshit. I'll tell him.

>   THEO *grabs her mother and pulls her downstage, hissing into her ear.*

ACT TWO

THEO: Mum, you're stoned.
BABS: Yes, I am rather.
THEO: Stop and count to—
JASPER: What's the big secret?

> BABS *turns and grins at* JASPER.

BABS: We all would've appreciated a little more notice, but … as it so happens, Theodora has—
THEO: Indigestion!
BABS: Indigestion, yes, caused by—
THEO: Flatulence!

> *She folds her arms across her belly and gives her mother an urgent glare.*

JASPER: That must be uncomfortable. [*Brightening*] Ah, cookies!
THEO / BABS: [*together*] No!

> *He takes a bite.*

JASPER: What has gotten into you two?

> WALLACE *storms in.*

WALLACE: Theo!
THEO: [*jumping*] Christ!
WALLACE: We *need* to talk.

> *He removes a little case from his back pocket and immediately opens it to reveal the wedding ring.*

JASPER: [*waving*] Hi, Wallace! Would you like a cookie?

> THEO *takes a pointed step in front of* WALLACE.

THEO: Mum, please …

> BABS *grabs the plate of cookies and makes sure she blocks* JASPER*'s view, half-wrestling him away from the action.*

BABS: [*to* JASPER] Why don't you go upstairs, love? Have a little kip. I'll see to dinner.
JASPER: [*with a shrug*] I guess I could meditate.
BABS: Yes, yes, you go up and chant.
JASPER: I've got this excellent new audio series. [*Calling*] Hey, Wallace … love the beard!

He goes.

WALLACE: Thanks, Grandpa!
THEO / BABS: [*together*] Grandpa?!
WALLACE: Well, he needs to find out somehow.
THEO: Wallace, go home.
WALLACE: But—
THEO: I'll be over in a minute. Just, go on ahead.

She pushes him out the door.

This room is spinning like the Gravitron.
BABS: You do look a little pink.

BABS bites into a cookie.

THEO: No more cookies, Babs!
BABS: You're such a square. [*Drifting*] Do people still say 'square'? I don't even know why it's insulting.

She draws a square in mid-air.

[*Pondering*] Square.
THEO: Come on.
BABS: I don't get it, do you?
THEO: Babs, I need you to be my mother again! [*She exhales.*] Everything's roasting. Is this what a hot flush feels like?
BABS: It's what a panic attack feels like.
THEO: Did Wallace just …?
BABS: He *almost* did.
THEO: Was that a genuine proposal? Holy fuck!
BABS: Language, Theodora!
THEO: I should go to him.
BABS: Wait. Just sit down for a moment. Catch your breath. Here, have some more tea.
THEO: I spiked the tea.
BABS: You what?
THEO: We were bonding!
BABS: It's like I'm living in a narcotics laboratory. [*Huffing*] And you with a baby and all.

JASPER's voice drifts down from upstairs. He's crooning to himself.

JASPER: [*singing*] Will you still love me tomoooorrow? Oh, oh, oh!
THEO: Do you have any idea what he's so happy about?
BABS: I shudder to think.

> THEO *reaches a decision.*

THEO: I'm going to catch up to Wallace. Don't worry, I'll be back in time for dinner.
BABS: Please don't pike on me.
THEO: I won't pike on you.

> *She gives her mother a kiss.*

BABS: Will you be engaged when you come back?

> BABS *bursts into tremors of laughter.*

THEO: Mum!
BABS: Sorry.
THEO: This is important.

> *Beat.*

> BABS *loses it again.*

BABS: [*cackling*] Wallace …
THEO: *Mum!*
BABS: It must suck to be you!
THEO: Nice. This is what I need right now.

> THEO *rushes out.*

BABS: [*calling after her*] Oh, can you pick up some broccoli? And an aubergine?
THEO: [*offstage*] What?
BABS: [*yelling*] *An auuuubergiiiiiine!*

> *Blackout.*

SCENE SIX

Darkness. Light slowly rises over the following …

CHAD: [*voiceover*] It's a simple con. I can't take credit for it. It's a system. A paradigm. A silent contract we've all agreed to without objection, without question and … for most of us … without any thought at all.

Spotlight on THEO, *touching her belly.*

[*Voiceover*] We start early. Right from the beginning, we tell our offspring that the possibilities are endless. They can be astronauts, they can be rock stars … hell, they can be both, they can sing 'Space Oddity' from beyond the earth's atmosphere if they just work hard enough. They can be supermodels, they can be President, they can be the next spiritual leader of Tibet! In fact, why work when you can wish? Wish as hard as you can!

Spotlight on JASPER, *eyes closed, meditating.*

[*Voiceover*] Everyone must believe that they are different and special, but few of us actually can be. The system relies on failure. After all, the global economy could never suffer the weight of seven billion billionaires.

CHAD *appears, in shadow.*

[*To the audience*] That's the beauty of it. That's what keeps the whole thing ticking! Expectation and failure. Failure and … [*grinning*] possibility. The highs, the lows. The 'maybes'. The 'if-onlys'. The 'what-ifs'!

The light continues to rise around him. Toxic words float and swell, and bleed.

So we buy books to help us 'maximise our potential'. We make vision boards and stare at them, really hard, hoping they'll come true! Maybe we'll be the one … the magic one … the blessed one. Because this world is so full of promise and someone, somewhere, has to cash in.

He steps directly into the light, resplendent in his snazziest suit. His voice echoes, punctuated by roaring thunder. The effect is nightmarish, surreal.

And, believe me, someone does. We all love a guru, right? That sacred success. That beacon. That prophet! Never mind that they're expensive, and that those who can't *do*, teach. The truth, ladies and gentleman, is that we'll cling to anyone who dangles a carrot. That's how you claw your way to the top. That's how you turn the great cosmic con to your advantage!

Smiling, he turns to regard first THEO *and then* JASPER. *He watches them both, shaking his head. A wolf shadow stretches out behind him.*

In the end, we're all whores for hope.

THEO *and* JASPER *fade.*

And no-one … nowhere … wants to be told that they're ordinary.

White strobes flicker.

SCENE SEVEN

THEO *crosses the stage, hidden beneath her hood and parka. Thunder purrs around her, but it is slowly, steadily, overwhelmed by the sound of an orchestra tuning.*

ANNI *crosses from the opposite direction, hidden beneath an identical hood and parka. She stops when she meets* THEO *and pushes the hood back, beaming.*

ANNI: Maestro!

She drops her parka. Beneath, she wears an elegant suit and tails.

Your audience is salivating!

From her top pocket, ANNI *withdraws a baton and places it in* THEO's *hand. Nonplussed, still hidden in her parka,* THEO *allows* ANNI *to guide her actions.*

Naturally, the music is right out there—Orff's 'O Fortuna' or Wagner's 'Ride of the Valkyries'—and ANNI *is loving it, closing her eyes as she forces* THEO *to wave the baton around.*

In the background, the rest of the cast appears in silhouette, some brandishing instruments or humming to the melody.

It's all coming together, or coming perfectly apart as it should, as it always must! What will you do now, Theo? Put a ring on it? Hmm? Slither back to Mummy and Daddy? This is the crisis point! *The crescendo!*

Lightning, thunder and hammering rain all compete with—and yet complement—the music. ANNI *laughs.*

We're gonna make 'em remember us. Our story will be a symphony!
THEO: *Enough!*

She drops the baton. The music succumbs to the sounds of the storm.

I don't want this, Anni. I don't want *any* of this.
ANNI: Urgh! Such a wet, pissy blanket.
THEO: It's just a life, okay? Just an ordinary—
ANNI: But we can make it so much more than ordinary! We can make it history, we can make it canon.
THEO: Canon?
ANNI: Or more ... we can make it beautiful.
THEO: Beauty is in the eye of—
ANNI: Everyone else! Grow up, Theo! If it hasn't been critiqued, if it hasn't been counted, then it can't have meaning. [*Softer*] I'm only trying to help.

She takes a step towards THEO.

THEO: Stay back.

Beat.

I have to deal with this alone.

ANNI *looks down at her toes as* THEO *exits. The music abruptly cuts out.*

ANNI: But you're not alone anymore.

Thunder rises, as a new track kicks in ...

SCENE EIGHT

Loud, contemporary hip hop music plays. FIGSBY *is dancing.* SASHA *has her face buried in a revolutionary magazine. A dejected* WALLACE *paces back and forth between them. Gradually, he starts trying on some moves, encouraged by* FIGSBY. *He's truly awful. Finally, he just can't take it anymore. He switches off the boombox.*

FIGSBY: Hey!
WALLACE: All these guys are singing about pimps. It's depressing.
FIGSBY: What do pimps even do?

ACT TWO

SASHA: [*indifferently*] They look after prostitutes.
FIGSBY: Like a shepherd?
SASHA: Kinda like a shepherd, yeah. [*Thinking*] Or sorta like an agent. You know, making connections, reeling in clients.

>   FIGSBY *considers this carefully.*

FIGSBY: How do they look after their prostitutes?
SASHA: They have heavies.
FIGSBY: Yeah, they'd need some heavies.

>   *Beat.*

>   WALLACE *lets out a sigh and looks down at the wedding ring in his hand.*

WALLACE: You two really don't have to stay. The conversation is scintillating, but—
FIGSBY: [*with a big smile*] We're here for you, hon.
WALLACE: Well, can you at least change the music? I'm trying to be dashing here. Whatever happened to good, wholesome, old-fashioned courtship? We need to bring back the classics, the romance.

>   *Beat.*

FIGSBY: Why don't the prostitutes just pretend to have a pimp?
WALLACE: What?
FIGSBY: Why don't they say, 'Yo, don't mess with me, I've got a pimp'.
SASHA: With some heavies?
FIGSBY: With some heavies, yeah.
SASHA: You definitely need the heavies.

>   *Beat.*

>   WALLACE *rubs his forehead. The stress is showing.*

FIGSBY: Do you wanna get a pizza?
WALLACE: No! I'm trying to make a memory here! This is the night when it all happens. This is the moment when I open my heart and let it pour into the woman I love.

>   SASHA *shuts her magazine.*

SASHA: Yuck.
WALLACE: It's beautiful!
SASHA: It's yuck.

WALLACE: I've found her. I've found the girl. She doesn't trust me to know that, but I do. I know how lucky I am and I know how special she is! I'm going to show her. I'm going to do this right, people. This is me taking the next step!

> FIGSBY *doesn't care. She has something far more serious on her mind.*

FIGSBY: They have a four cheese pizza now.

> *She holds up her fingers and eyeballs* WALLACE, *straight-faced and solemn.*

Four cheeses.

WALLACE: [*deflated*] Alright, we'll order a fucking pizza.

> *He starts pacing once again, leaving* FIGSBY *to dial.*

Where is she? [*Worried*] Maybe she didn't like the ring.

> *He holds it up for inspection.*

It's nice, isn't it?

FIGSBY: [*distracted*] Gorgeous.

WALLACE: It *is* gorgeous.

SASHA: [*bored*] Classy.

WALLACE: That's right! I'm a classy guy! [*A little desperate*] Should I text her?

> SASHA *stifles a yawn.*

[*Ignoring her*] What should I say? I can't write 'Will you marry me?' in a text, can I? [*Urgently*] Can I?

> *No response.*

I can't believe I'm asking my friends for editorial advice on a text message.

> SASHA *stands.*

SASHA: Wallace, you need to prepare yourself for the ... tragic probability that you may not be her dream specimen.

WALLACE: [*stone cold*] Hey, I'm her dream.

SASHA: Really?

WALLACE: Really really.

FIGSBY: [*scoffing*] Really?

ACT TWO

WALLACE: *Really!*

SASHA: Mr and Mrs Bobbottom. It's not attractive.

WALLACE: [*downcast*] She can keep her family name.

SASHA: *You* need to keep your toe behind the party line, Wallace.

WALLACE: Sash, listen … that's the sound of nobody caring what you think.

SASHA: You're the voice of the future, you lizardy jizzrocket! Don't you dare throw it away for some chick who doesn't even want—

WALLACE: Hey, she wants!

SASHA: [*looking him up and down*] She wants … this?

WALLACE: She wants *all* of this. Sixty-two kilograms of raw passion!

He puffs himself up. SASHA *takes out a packet of cigarettes.*

SASHA: I'm just saying, it may not be as good for her as it is for—

WALLACE *snatches the packet before she can light up.*

Oi!

WALLACE: Figsby!

He throws the cigarettes to FIGSBY, *who immediately bins the packet and returns fire by throwing a lollipop at* WALLACE.

SASHA: *Give that—!*

WALLACE *shoves the lollipop straight into* SASHA*'s mouth.*

Beat.

WALLACE: Better?

She nods, peevishly.

Now I know neither of you are onboard, but this thing—Theo and Wallace, happily ever after—it's happening!

SASHA *gestures with her eyes.*

What?

She does it again.

[*Turning*] Figsby, what is her …?

THEO *has entered, catching* WALLACE *off guard. She is still wearing her ridiculous parka and holds a shopping bag in each hand.*

> WALLACE *gapes at her, speechless.*

THEO: Why the fuck would you want to get married?
WALLACE: [*hangdog*] I thought it might be nice.
THEO: [*shaking her head*] I'm sorry.

> SASHA *takes out her lollipop.*

SASHA: Heh! Told you, buttmunch!

> WALLACE *sticks it back in her mouth.*

THEO: Are you angry with me?
WALLACE: No, not really.
THEO: Not really? So you *are* angry with me?
WALLACE: I'm fine. I'm merry. Just leave it.
THEO: Is it what you truly want? Marriage? Instant family, just add water? There's no coming back from that, Wallace.
WALLACE: Why don't you be honest with me, tell me what I've done wrong and give me a chance to apologise?
THEO: …
WALLACE: I don't want you to hate me.
THEO: I don't hate you. I like you. A lot. That's why I'm hot and cold with you.
WALLACE: That's stupid.
THEO: It makes sense if you think about it.
WALLACE: No, it's hormonal logic. [*To* FIGSBY] Can you believe this?
FIGSBY: I'm not getting involved.
WALLACE: She's shirty with me because she finds me attractive.
THEO: And he's *pissy* with me because I won't agree to a shotgun wedding.
FIGSBY: [*rolling her eyes*] He likes you, you like him. Why do white people have to complain all the time?
WALLACE: That's an offensive generalisation.
SASHA: Oh boo hoo, Wallace.
FIGSBY: [*to* WALLACE] You're my best friend, I just want you to stop planning your life and start living it.
WALLACE: I'm trying to be the mature one!
THEO: So am I!

> *They both turn to* FIGSBY *for support.*

ACT TWO

FIGSBY: I'm not your referee.

> SASHA *pulls the lollipop from her mouth and waves it with authority.*

SASHA: Well, *I* have a few thoughts. [*To* THEO] First of all, you're a ten, but Wallace is like a two, two and a half ...
THEO: Back up a second! Turn around. What's with all the pregnancy kits? [*Peering*] There must be half a dozen here.
FIGSBY: [*proudly*] A whole dozen!
WALLACE: Figsby has a supplier.
SASHA: And I have a baseball bat and a lorry van.
THEO: [*frowning*] Figsby?
WALLACE: Yeah, I know, she's named after a fruit ... you're named after a vegetable.
FIGSBY: I just like the way they taste.

> FIGSBY *gently brushes* WALLACE *aside and draws close to* THEO.

THEO: [*smiling*] Theodora Sprout.
FIGSBY: Imani Fisseha Azikiwe.

> *She touches* THEO*'s hand.*

THEO: That's pretty.

> THEO *is spellbound.*
>
> *Beat.*
>
> WALLACE *clears his throat.*

WALLACE: [*pointing*] And this is Sash, my campaign manager. She's a little ... well, she's a fascist.
SASHA: Oi!
WALLACE: I wouldn't say it's like working with Hitler exactly, but one of the top five ...

> SASHA *raps his head with her lollipop while he cries out.*

Goebbels! [*Cringing*] Or Mengele! [*Yelping*] ... Or Ilse Koch!
THEO: Pleasure to meet you both.
FIGSBY: Yes, it is!

> *She grins.*

Do you dance, Theodora?

WALLACE: Stop … enthralling my lady friend.
FIGSBY: [*innocently*] I'm being sociable.
WALLACE: Figsby was just about to order a pizza.
FIGSBY: [*serene*] No.
WALLACE: [*tensely*] Figsby. Was. Just. About. To. Order—

> THEO *turns on him.*

THEO: *Twelve* pregnancy kits! Twelve!
WALLACE: She got carried away.
THEO: Did she? Or did you?

> SASHA *gives* WALLACE *one final lollipop-smack, before beaming at* THEO.

WALLACE: It's important to cover our bases.
THEO: Right, you just wanted to be sure, to be sure, to be sure, to be sure, to be sure—
WALLACE: I don't know what I'm doing, okay? We're in uncharted woods. It's dark and scary. I know you feel it too.
THEO: So you expect me to submit to your little home science experiment?
WALLACE: It's just a—a 'medical technicality.
THEO: And if the stick turns blue you want Dad to shimmy me down the aisle?
WALLACE: That's the plan. Is it so wrong?
SASHA: [*to* FIGSBY] Wait … is she actually up the duff?
FIGSBY: I think he did it.
THEO: Fuck, Wallace! You call yourself a revolutionary, but as soon as you encounter the unexpected you rewind to the nineteen fifties.
WALLACE: Theo, since when have you been a—

> *All three women turn and eyeball* WALLACE.

[*Meekly*] Historian.
THEO: Don't tell me I'm not a feminist just because I separate the real issues from the nonsense ones. This is *my* life, my body!
WALLACE: *Our* life! [*He swallows.*] Our life, Theo.

> *She turns away from him.*

> FIGSBY *looks down at her own toes.* SASHA, *speechless at last, averts her eyes and focuses on her lollipop.*

ACT TWO

Tell me what you need.

Long beat.

THEO *turns back to face* WALLACE.

THEO: I need *someone* to be ordinary.
WALLACE: …
THEO: No drama, no agenda … just … ordinary.
WALLACE: I can do that.

SASHA takes the lollipop out of her mouth to speak, but WALLACE *cuts her off before she can.*

I so can!
FIGSBY: Here's a radical idea: why don't you stop trying to marry this woman and start kissing her instead?

WALLACE *walks up to* THEO, *a little timid.*

THEO: Relax. I'll take the lead.

She kisses him.

Don't play with me.

She kisses him again.

I mean it, don't play with me.
WALLACE: But I want to play with you.
THEO: Don't propose because you think you have to. Either you feel something or—
WALLACE: Theo, you've been my obsession since the day we met. No, actually, since the day I saw you passing on a school bus. It took one drive-by for me to be utterly smitten.

Beat.

THEO: [*grinning*] Okay, you can play with me now.

They kiss again …

FIGSBY *shudders all over*

I love it when our bodies are pressed together.
WALLACE: It works better when you're not wearing a parka.

SASHA *gags.*

[*Smiling*] Should I boot them out?

THEO: Babs sent me to fetch dinner supplies. I'd like to ravish you. [*With a melodramatic sigh*] The spirit wants to do naughty things. Special parts of my body want to do naughty things. But I can barely walk.
WALLACE: Okay, you lie still ... I'll just go for it.
FIGSBY: *Guys!*

They turn.

You're like a pair of wildebeests! [*Re: phone*] These people keep putting me on hold. Listen to this.

She presses a button. Susan Boyle plays.

THEO: Jesus! That woman *must* be stopped!

THEO *snatches the phone and switches it off.*

FIGSBY: Hey, what about my pizza? Nooo!
THEO: Come back to mine. Babs will make enough for everybody.
WALLACE: I guess our ravishing plan is out the window. It was a good plan. [*Wistful*] A wise plan.
THEO: You think you're so charming and irresistible that I might change my mind and decide I want to stay?

She thinks.

Well, you are and I could, but something's up with Dad. Something new.
WALLACE: Bloody Jasper. [*Smiling optimistically*] Are you sure you don't want to pee before we go?
THEO: Twelve times?
WALLACE: Once would remove our doubts.
THEO: There are no doubts.

She opens her parka and pats her belly.

WALLACE: *Holy crispy crap!*
SASHA: [*shuddering*] Put that away, it's revolting!

Everyone stares.

THEO: You're not very good with anatomy are you, Wallace? [*Quickly*] But don't you dare get down on one knee again. It's a goldfish, remember?
SASHA: That's not a goldfish, it's a parasite!
FIGSBY: Are you sure it's just one?!
THEO: We'll figure it out. We don't have to panic.

ACT TWO

WALLACE: [*frozen*] Okay.

> *Beat.*

SASHA: Um … congratulations?
WALLACE: [*swallowing*] Cheers.
FIGSBY: You still owe me for all of these boxes, and the water.
THEO: [*grinning*] Fetch your coats, boys and girls.

> THEO *picks up her shopping and heads for the door.* WALLACE *blinks, snapping out of his stupor.*

WALLACE: Theo …

> *Beat.*

I like goldfish.

> *She nods slowly. Understanding passes between them.*

THEO: Me too.

> *Blackout.*

SCENE NINE

BABS *appears in a spotlight. She's wearing her oven mitts.*

BABS: [*calling*] Are you coming down, cherry cake?!

> *Another spot lights up, revealing* JASPER, *his back to the audience. He sprays cologne.*

JASPER: [*calling back*] Just gimme five!

> *They freeze as* THEO *appears, in her newest, snazziest gingham dress. She weaves between them.*

THEO: The board is set, as they say.

> *Another spot lights up, downstage.* WALLACE, FIGSBY *and* SASHA *are frozen too, midway through the act of putting on their coats.*

You might think I'm a glutton for punishment. Hell, you might even think I'm certifiably insane for letting Wallace back into my house when he still has that ring in his back pocket. But sometimes you've gotta stop biting your tongue and tiptoeing around. Sometimes you've gotta bring things to a head. [*Shrugging*] I can't be a mummy till I sort out my daddy issues.

THEO *takes note of the people in her life. They all remain motionless in separate—and distinctly coloured—pools of light.*

[*To her belly*] This is our family. For better or for worse. Mostly it's for the better. We clash. We confuse each other. We say cruel things. But, nobody knows us the way we know us. In our tiny corner of the world, we are the stars of our own little soap opera. For me that's enough to build a life around. Who'd want to be any more famous than that?

Music kicks in.

Slowly, the figures in spotlights begin to move. They go about their business in half-speed. The song 'Fame' (David Bowie) plays as the spots break up into showbiz searchlights. The figures move languidly, drifting through a dream space.

They dress the set.

The baby grand piano resumes pride of place, the mirror ball spins above and the characters greet each other with exaggerated gestures.

JASPER *is dressed to party, clapping* WALLACE *on the back and pawing* BABS. FIGSBY *dances.* SASHA *picks at the hors d'oeuvres.* BABS *struggles to set the table.*

Only THEO *is removed from the scene, watching off to one side.*

A doorbell rings. The spell is broken.

Lights change.

SCENE TEN

THEO *smooths down her dress.*

THEO: I'll get it.

She opens the door and takes her first look at CHAD …

Instant revulsion.

CHAD: Ah, excellent …

He extends a hand.

… you must be Theodora. [*Grinning*] I'm Chad.

ACT TWO

THEO: [*yelling over her shoulder*] Mum, one of your God botherers has followed you home!

> BABS *takes a look.*

BABS: He's not one of mine.

> JASPER *makes a beeline for the door, shoving* WALLACE *as he goes.*

JASPER: Hey man! So glad you could come. [*To the room*] Everyone, this is Chad Mombardo. [*Proudly*] My guide in this reality.

THEO: [*rolling her eyes*] Awwwww, Mary wept.

JASPER: [*to* CHAD] We're *all* pleased to see you. [*Tersely, eyeballing* THEO] Every single one of us.

CHAD: Great! I brought—

JASPER: A red! My favourite!

CHAD: Actually, it's—

JASPER: Champagne, whatever!

> *He takes the bottle.*

How was the drive?

CHAD: Well, I—

JASPER: It's a pretty smooth run now that the expressway has two lanes.

CHAD: —caught the bus.

JASPER: Oh. Cool.

> *Awkward beat.*

[*Pointing*] This is my missus. Babs.

BABS: [*confused*] Barbara Sprout ... How do you do?

> CHAD *opens his mouth to respond.* JASPER *steamrolls right over him.*

JASPER: And you've met the sprog.

THEO: *Dad!*

JASPER: Sorry. [*Looking at her*] Go easy on the cookies tonight, Theo.

> *Beat.*

BABS: Theodora, why don't you take the gentleman's ... what is that garment?

CHAD: It's a Chilean chamanto.

BABS: Oh, it's rather ... are you from Chile?

CHAD: Melbourne.
BABS: I see.

>Beat.

THEO: Do you want it gone?
CHAD: Please.

>THEO *takes it away.*

BABS: Jasper has quite a collection of exotic coats. He has a chuba and a poncho.
CHAD: [*smirking*] A poncho is the poor man's chamanto.

>JASPER *laughs, a little too urgently.* CHAD *is chuffed and breaks into a broad smile.*

JASPER: Isn't he terrific? [*To* CHAD] You're terrific!

>*The laughter dies off, leaving an agonising pause in its wake.*

CHAD: [*clearing his throat*] Thank you …
JASPER: You're welcome.
CHAD: … for having me. [*To* BABS] Jasper has shared many enticing details about his home life.
BABS: He has?
CHAD: Oh, indeed. I can feel a distinct energy in this room. It's very positive, very stimulating.
THEO: It is?
CHAD: Yes, yes … very 'up'.
FIGSBY: I know what you mean, Chad. [*To* WALLACE] I feel like I've been here before.

>CHAD *feeds from* FIGSBY*'s enthusiasm.*

CHAD: I'd call it a warm energy, wouldn't you? Not quite orange, but … [*snapping his fingers*] ochre!
BABS: [*taking it in*] Ochre …

>*She nods, not all that confidently.*

CHAD: There's an instant rush in a happy home. It oozes from the walls, from the carpet, from the—
FIGSBY: Hey! I *do* know this place. This is Shred Lord's place!

>SASHA *lights up.*

SASHA: Riiiight! I had a drummer on that bench top.

ACT TWO

CHAD: [*thrown*] You ... had a drummer?
SASHA: [*pointing*] On that bench top!

> *She flutters her eyelashes, making fun of* CHAD's *naivety.*

It's a *very* happy home, Mrs. Sprout.

> JASPER *and* BABS *share an awkward look.*

BABS: [*too cheerful*] Perhaps we should all sit down. I'm afraid dinner will be a teensy weensy while. Would anyone care for a cup of tea? If you're feeling devilish, we have the Super Spiced Chai ... but it's not for the faint-hearted.
CHAD: That sounds lovely, Barbara.
THEO: Dad ... a word!

> *She pulls* JASPER *downstage left.*

Where did you pick up that dummy?
JASPER: He's an intelligent, well-travelled—
THEO: I don't mean 'dummy' as in stupid ... I mean 'dummy' as in soulless, synthetic lump masquerading as a human being.
JASPER: Just be civil for one night, Theo.
THEO: I'm always civil.
JASPER: Okay, then try to be a bit groovy, a bit ... hip.
THEO: Hip?
JASPER: Yeah!
THEO: Dad, I don't know what that means. In fact, I have it on good authority that it's hip to be square, and I think I *might* be square, so ...
JASPER: Alright, alright, pretend that *I'm* hip. Look up to me.
THEO: I do look up—
JASPER: For example! [*Pointing*] Can you get those girls to laugh at my jokes? Especially the black one!
THEO: Excuse me?
JASPER: She's very cool. [*Watching* FIGSBY] They're all a bit cool, aren't they?
THEO: Dad, I'm really feeling the generation gap tonight.
JASPER: Okay. Forget it.

> *He seems to accept that he's out of line ... for a second.*

The ginger, then.
THEO: What?

JASPER: I need a groupie.

THEO: *Dad?!*

JASPER: I mean a fan! A platonic fan! [*Serious*] Do you think they'd be into my Neil Diamond collection?

THEO: My friends are not for sale.

JASPER: It's important to me!

THEO: But, why?

JASPER: Because this little social occasion could have a massive impact on my career.

THEO: What career?

JASPER: Wow!

THEO: What?

JASPER: That's just … wow, that's … so cold, Theo.

THEO: I don't know what we're talking about!

JASPER: You've never seen me.

THEO: Huh?

JASPER: I've raised you, I've clothed you … or tried … I would never have suggested gingham …

THEO: Why are you so outraged?

JASPER: I've imparted my knowledge, shared my beliefs …

THEO: I'm still not getting it.

JASPER: But you've never *seen* me, Theo. You've never appreciated the extent of my capacity for self-actualisation.

    Beat.

    A frustrated squeal from THEO.

  Oh, go on … wail … wail away!

THEO: You are so deluded! I don't know what's worse: the fact that you truly believe there's still a geriatric's chance in hell that you will *ever* expand on your shining five and a half minutes of fame, or the fact that you dare … *you dare* … to assert that Mum and I fail to see you, hear you, smell you, breathe you and think you, you, *you* all the freakin' time!

JASPER: Theo—

    A loud screech from THEO.

  Theo, I only meant—

ACT TWO

THEO: 'Ego' doesn't come close … 'superego' doesn't even cover it … they haven't invented a scale for your level of conceit. Your 'id' is off the chart!
JASPER: One night! Help me … humour me … for just one night!
THEO: Fine!

>   *Beat.* THEO *shoves her belly in his face.*

Guess what, dickhead? I'm pregnant.

>   *She rejoins the party, leaving* JASPER *stunned.*

>   *Elsewhere,* BABS *is pouring tea.*

BABS: Now, I caution you to sip slowly. This spice is quite wicked.
CHAD: I'm not afraid. Fear leads to anger.
WALLACE: [*smiling*] Right.
CHAD: Problem?
WALLACE: You're quoting, aren't you?
CHAD: No.

>   *He sips.*

[*To* BABS] Divine. Simply divine.

>   *Beat.*

I think I recognise your little friend here.

>   *He gestures to the altar.*

Egyptian, obviously. [*He snaps his fingers.*] Is it Ra?
BABS: No, his mother.

>   *She smiles at* THEO.

Hathor is the goddess of joy, feminine love and fertility. Sometimes she is depicted as a mother and other times as a daughter. In either case, she is the herald of imminent birth.
CHAD: I see.
BABS: Everyone is fixated on Ra, but he only controls the sun. This fine lady rules over all the other stars in the Milky Way. [*With a grin*] I bought her for only thirty-nine ninety-five on Gumtree.

>   CHAD *holds his grin.*

CHAD: Mothers are too often undervalued.

> BABS *catches* CHAD *in her eyes. There is fire in them.*

So, Wallace, what field are you in?
WALLACE: Field?
CHAD: Business.
WALLACE: Oh, I'm … a troll.
CHAD: How's that working out for you?

> THEO *squeezes her boyfriend's shoulder.*

THEO: Wallace doesn't need any of your advice, Mr Mombardo.
CHAD: Chad.

> *He returns his cup to the saucer and studies* THEO, *slipping easily into another cold smile.*

Everyone needs guidance from time to time. Even you, I'm sure.
THEO: I prefer to be an adult.

> *She offers* CHAD *a cookie.* BABS, *horrified, slaps it out of her hand.* CHAD's *smile freezes over. His eyes dart to* FIGSBY, *who shrinks back a little.*

CHAD: What about you, Frisbee?
THEO: It's Figsby.
CHAD: [*ignoring her*] Are you full … inside?
FIGSBY: [*thrown*] I'm looking forward to pudding.
CHAD: Well, I mean … is there someone special waiting for you at home?
FIGSBY: [*with a shrug*] Grandma.
CHAD: I see. No doubt Theo can give you some pointers when it comes to the rougher sex.

> *He turns back to face* THEO, *waving his hand at her belly.*

She's been … productive.

> THEO *winces at this, but maintains her cool.*

THEO: [*patting* WALLACE] I met this pus rag online.
CHAD: The Internet! Ingenious!
SASHA: [*to* FIGSBY] They do give you a discount if you have a vagina.

> *She raises her hand for a high five.* BABS *slaps it, absently.*

FIGSBY: Perhaps I'm happy with the way things are, Mr Mombardo.

ACT TWO

People are far more complicated than your little slogans would have us all believe.
CHAD: No, this is good. This is meaty stuff. I gather you're somewhat … [*making rabbit ears*] 'political'.
FIGSBY: I like to contribute, yes.
CHAD: Our very own Black Panther.
FIGSBY: Actually I'm a Girl Scout from Burnside, but keep digging.
SASHA: We were comrades in arms until Wallace got all fluffy and tender on us. At least we know what we represent.

WALLACE has helped himself to the plate of dope cookies.

WALLACE: [*woozily, with mouth full*] What is *that* supposed to mean?
SASHA: You're bailing on us. Going soft, mate.
WALLACE: I've always been soft, but I'm not bailing.

He reaches for the last crumb. THEO *hangs her head.*

SASHA: Soft like peanut butter. Like baby wipes!
WALLACE: Hey, I'm still at the top of the ticket.
SASHA: For now, spunkbubble.
WALLACE: Tyrant!
SASHA: Asstaxi!
WALLACE: Adolf Titler!
CHAD: Take it down, take it down.

He soothes them with his smile.

Your feelings do you credit. [*Leaning forward*] But is your heart empty? Is there a space, a void, that needs …

THEO *laughs.*

Yes?
THEO: Sorry, but … come on! This isn't analysis, this isn't depth … we're not bonding here.
BABS: Manners, Theodora.

CHAD *holds up his hand.* BABS *bites her lip.*

CHAD: I'm sensing a wall between us.
THEO: You don't say.
CHAD: I think it's *your* wall, Theodora.
THEO: My wall?

CHAD: Yes, I think you have a large wall built all around you. You've turned your heart into a citadel.
THEO: [*laughing*] And you're a fucking fortune cookie.
CHAD: Shall we ask your friends? [*To* WALLACE] Do you believe Theodora is open and unguarded in all her dealings with you?

> WALLACE *looks away.* THEO*'s mirth evaporates.*

THEO: That's not fair.
CHAD: Come on, Wally … [*Cruelly*] Don't be shy.
BABS: I'll check on the lasagne!
JASPER: [*waving*] Babs …

> BABS *joins* JASPER, *who hasn't moved since* THEO *dropped her bomb.*

BABS: Why are you loitering all the way over here? That horrible man is *your* guest.
JASPER: Theo is … [*swooning*] … she … she just told me …
BABS: Oh? [*Getting it*] Oh!
JASPER: My girl.
BABS: Take a seat.
JASPER: My precious girl.
BABS: I know.
JASPER: She's with child.
BABS: Hush now. I should've expected her to turn her secret into a weapon. We've raised a very resourceful little chook together, haven't we?
JASPER: Who did this? I'll castrate the bastard!

> BABS *points.*
>
> *Beat.*

Wallace? [*Blinking*] Little Wallace?
BABS: [*nodding*] Apparently he managed it.
JASPER: No … nooo, he must be covering for someone.
BABS: They appear to be very much in love.
JASPER: She's in love with Wallace?
BABS: I'm afraid so, dear.
JASPER: Little Wallace with the turkey legs and the landing strip on his face?

> BABS *puts her arm around him.*

ACT TWO

BABS: My poor chipmunk, this isn't your best day ever, is it?

>THEO *storms downstage right.* WALLACE *hurries after her.*

WALLACE: You're letting him get to you.

THEO: Why aren't you standing up for me, Wallace?

WALLACE: I *am* standing up for you ... just not in a fighty way, more of a standy way.

THEO: He's a monster!

WALLACE: He's a carnival magician. Look at him. Rat-faced fuck.

THEO: We're supposed to be a team!

WALLACE: We *are* a team!

>*His tummy growls.*

Theo?

THEO: Yeah.

WALLACE: Did you bake your 'naughty' cookies?

THEO: [*meekly*] You look really hot tonight.

WALLACE: Theo!

>BABS *taps her spoon against a teacup.*

BABS: Places, everyone! I'm about to serve.

WALLACE: [*swooning*] Your mum is so much like Mary Poppins.

THEO: She's uncomfortable.

WALLACE: That makes ... [*looking around*] ... all of us. [*Staring at nothing*] I feel like we should hug. Just one big, sexy group squeeze.

BABS: Places, places.

>*Everyone sits around the table.* THEO *and* CHAD *share a glare as they take their seats, immediately upstaged by* JASPER'*s steelier, nastier glare aimed directly at an oblivious* WALLACE.
>
>*Clouds churn and form ominous shapes. Lightning slashes through the sky ... words pass like knives. The tension is searing.*

WALLACE: So what, exactly, is your job, Mr ... Chad?

JASPER: He's my mentor. You could use one of those, Wallace. Someone to keep you on the straight and narrow. Make sure you're thinking with your head and not with ... my daughter's tail.

>THEO *kicks her leg out under the table.*

FIGSBY: Ow!

THEO: Pass that on to my father.

JASPER: [*smirking*] Of course it takes two to tango … and to get jiggy wit' it.

THEO: You're always telling me to let go of my inhibitions, aren't you?

JASPER: Even the sixties had their limits.

THEO: You're always telling me to explore myself.

JASPER: If you were exploring yourself, we wouldn't be having this conversation.

> *Beat.*

CHAD: I'm sensing some veiled hostility here. Maybe we should all breathe together.

THEO: Do you think my father is looking a little long in the tooth? And in the gut?

CHAD: [*warily*] No, I wouldn't say that.

THEO: You sure? I think it's time to add a cardie to that exotic coat collection.

JASPER: I feel wonderful.

THEO: Not tired?

JASPER: Spritely.

THEO: But the bags under your eyes, and all those grey prickles in your beard.

JASPER: You're only as old as you feel.

THEO: Those are serious Steve Martin prickles.

JASPER: You're being childish.

THEO: Then you must teach me, wise old man.

> *The glares continue.*

BABS: Isn't this festive?

> *She downs her glass.*

More wine? [*Rising*] I'll crack open another bottle.

> THEO *gropes for her, but* BABS—*mouthing an apology—wriggles away and makes a run for it.*

JASPER: I hope you're happy with yourself. She can't take the stress.

THEO: She's the strongest person in this family.

JASPER: [*to* WALLACE] I'm looking at you, JFK … this wasn't part of my life plan! [*Whining*] Why couldn't you keep it in your jockey shorts?

ACT TWO

Beat.

WALLACE: [*to* CHAD] So … you're in sales?
CHAD: I'm a source of inspiration, Wallace.
THEO: And how much does that cost?

> JASPER *kicks out under the table.*

FIGSBY: Ow!
JASPER: Pass it back.

> CHAD *peers into the bread basket and picks at the loaf within.*

CHAD: A human being is measured by his accomplishments. Many of us, however, fail to move ahead with our life plan as swiftly and as effectively as we would like. We struggle to optimise our triumph quotient. I help to arouse that process.

> *He bites into the bread.*

THEO: Basically, you're a cheerleader.
CHAD: Plus I make direct connections for my clients. Not *all* of my clients, you understand. The special ones.
JASPER: [*grinning*] I'm a special one.
CHAD: Amen.

> *They turn their smug smiles on* THEO.

FIGSBY: I get it now. [*To* WALLACE] He's a pimp!

> THEO *smirks back at them.*

CHAD: Perhaps you would all appreciate a little demonstration of my extraordinary insight?
THEO: It's the modesty that really sells it.
CHAD: Modesty is for the mediocre. [*To* SASHA] Young miss, I couldn't help but notice that you have a …

> *He plucks the lollipop from* SASHA*'s mouth.*

 … habit. [*Gesturing*] Do you mind?

> SASHA *eyes* CHAD *with hostility as he beckons to her. When she fails to resist, however, he helps her out of her chair and theatrically removes her coat. Her arms and shoulders are covered in nicotine patches.*

I thought so. [*Beaming*] Knew so, in fact.

SASHA: Hey, I'm off the fags, but the patches are sweet. They give you a nice, even rush.
CHAD: The problem is not the 'fags' or the patches.

He draws close.

The problem, young miss, lies here.

He touches her forehead.

SASHA: [*mesmerised*] Wow ... so you're what happens when ferrets get horny.
CHAD: So tense. [*Gently*] Someone hurt you, didn't they?
SASHA: Someone hurts everyone.
CHAD: But you must move forward, young miss. Don't let your past become a cage.
SASHA: I bet your booty gets real jealous when all that shit pours out of your mouth.

But it's working. SASHA *is losing her edge.* CHAD *places his arm over her.*

CHAD: Are you acquainted with Maslow's Hierarchy of Needs ...? Safety, belonging, esteem, self-actualisation.
FIGSBY: Where I come from, people just want a glass of water.
CHAD: [*ignoring her*] Your needs are sacred.
THEO: Sacred, right. This is how selfishness becomes a religion. [*To* JASPER] Are you catching on yet?
JASPER: Be careful.
THEO: He's just like every bad manager you've ever signed on with except he dances before he fucks you.

JASPER *slams his cutlery down.*

JASPER: *Theo, that's enough!*

Beat.

THEO *is chastised.*

SASHA *takes a step closer to* CHAD.

SASHA: [*shrewdly*] So what can you do for me?

CHAD *spreads his arms wide, taking in the world.*

THEO *can't believe her eyes. She is about to storm away from the table when—*

ACT TWO

BABS *returns with dinner.*

BABS: Here we are. Guest goes first.

> FIGSBY *raises her plate expectantly, cutting* CHAD *off. Cool as ever,* CHAD *takes it in his stride.*

CHAD: [*to* BABS] Jasper tells me you two met on the dance floor.
BABS: He was all about the hips.
JASPER: [*relaxing*] And she was all about the panty line.
BABS: I was a chubby teenager … it wasn't a panty line, it was an extreme crevice.
JASPER: [*with a laugh*] She was beautiful then, and she's perfect now.

> THEO *bangs her fist against the table.*

THEO: She's your wife, not a holiday destination.
WALLACE: Easy, Theo. [*Earnestly*] It's love.
THEO: When was the last time you ever put the kettle on for her?
JASPER: When was the last time you ever gave me a compliment?

> CHAD *gestures for calm.*

CHAD: I think this hostility is becoming … less veiled. [*To* THEO] You're piling some extra bricks on top of those walls tonight, aren't you dear?
THEO: I hate you.
CHAD: Is it envy, perhaps? Your father is an artist. Part of a select breed. [*To* JASPER, *with a nod*] An elite club!
WALLACE: [*sheepishly*] Pass the mayonnaise …?
CHAD: [*doing so*] You can hardly demand that he be here for you all the time and you certainly can't expect him to go out and 'get a job' like an ordinary human being.
THEO: He *is* an ordinary human being!
CHAD: Watch it, you'll stifle him.

> JASPER *sighs.*

JASPER: Theo, our miscommunication can be testing, but maybe … [*Off* CHAD'*s look*] in fact *probably* … we shouldn't deny that I *am* different from you, and it is only natural that I embrace—
THEO: Try English. I don't speak dipshit.
CHAD: There are some people who are *meant* to wait tables and scan groceries, and some who are … I'm just going to put it out there … exceptional.

THEO: I hate you!
CHAD: [*perfectly cheerful*] You said that already.

> *Beat.*

BABS: This hasn't cooked all the way through has it? The centre is stone cold. [*With forced cheer*] Silly chef!

> *She laughs. Nobody responds.*

> FIGSBY *nudges* WALLACE, *gesturing for him to intervene.* WALLACE *tries to resist, then reluctantly lowers his fork.*

WALLACE: [*with forced cheer*] Well, I've always enjoyed Jasper's voice.
SASHA: If you ask me, there's nothing wrong with having a teacher.
THEO: Oh, so he's a teacher now?
FIGSBY: [*with a shrug*] Those who can't do, teach. Those who can't teach, preach.
THEO: A teacher—a *real* teacher—is someone who cares for their student. Someone who not only has knowledge, but understanding. [*Pointing to* BABS] That woman is my teacher.

> BABS *half-smiles, half-shrinks from all the attention.*

BABS: I'm flattered, darling … but I'm hardly qualified.
THEO: You're wise, you're kind and you give a damn.
CHAD: It takes a little more than good intentions to get by in this world.
THEO: Chad … may I call you Chad?
CHAD: Please.

> THEO *puts her fork down.*

THEO: Chad, when you first invaded my family home I thought you were a shark. I see now that I gave you far too much respect. You're not a shark … you're a remora.
BABS: [*guarded*] What's a remora, dear?
THEO: Those are the pathetic midget fish that follow sharks around all the time. They never leave them alone.
JASPER: Now, Theo—
THEO: They cling to them. [*Enjoying herself*] They suck up to them. Bottom feeders.
FIGSBY: [*her mouth full*] Parasites.
THEO: Parasites! Thank you, Figsby.
FIGSBY: No problem.

ACT TWO 101

THEO: You, Chad, are a parasite.
CHAD: Am I? What an intriguing notion.

He dabs his mouth with a napkin. All of his easy charm vaporises.

Your father was a star before you were born. He was going somewhere ... everywhere ... and then there was a hungry little mouth yelping his name, draining his wallet ... [*grunting*] wasting his time.

The room becomes very cold.

You're right, of course. Time is not only valuable, it's critical. Time and youth. Your father is running out of both, as you so eagerly observe, but I am not the creature that has taken them from him. I didn't sap his energy and swallow his best years. That was all you. [*Smiling*] All of it.

He calmly resumes his meal. Everyone stares as CHAD *takes a delicate bite. The wallpaper writhes. Lightning flares.*

I'm not a parasite, Theodora ... and I will never, ever be a small fish.

THEO *drops her fork and, finally, leaves the table. She makes her way downstage, holding back tears. It isn't long before she has fallen completely to her knees.*

WALLACE *and* BABS *both stand, but it is* JASPER *who runs over to her. The room is losing substance. Furniture melts.* CHAD, *grinning wolfishly, is bathed in fumes.*

JASPER: Theo—
CHAD: Wait.

He drops a hand firmly onto JASPER'*s shoulder. Red lights slowly rise.*

This is your test, Jasper. [*Smiling*] Mine as well.

He steers JASPER *back to the table.*

Do you think I enjoy being this honest? Theo has her own life to lead ... and it will be a beautiful life ... but you, my friend, must answer a higher calling.

JASPER *glances over his shoulder at* THEO. CHAD *waits, knowing* JASPER *will bite. His shadow stretches over them all.*

JASPER: What do you mean?

CHAD: [*pouncing*] As an artist, you owe it to the public to realise your full potential. It would be selfish to deprive them.

Still smiling, CHAD *tops up* JASPER*'s glass.*

As your mentor, it falls on me to shepherd you through this transition. Great artists need to rise above the average, and that means leaving the little things behind.

BABS: [*quietly appalled*] The little things?

CHAD: Sacrifices are essential.

He returns JASPER*'s glass.*

Art is suffering.

JASPER: [*repeating the mantra*] 'Art is suffering.' [*Spellbound*] I never knew that.

WALLACE *snorts and* BABS *sighs, but* CHAD *has the floor.*

CHAD: How much do you know of the great scribes? Orwell—outcast! Hemingway—manic depressive! And let's not even get started on Plath!

SASHA: What happened to Plath?

CHAD: Head in the oven!

JASPER: But I just want to make people happy.

CHAD *nods in sympathy, cogs turning all the while.*

CHAD: Shakespeare! [*He snaps his fingers.*] Shakespeare knew he couldn't balance his art with his family, so he let them go!

He is pacing now, taking the group in.

Oh, I'm sure it tore him in two, but if he had chosen fatherhood over his calling we would all be poorer for it.

JASPER: [*to himself*] Theo doesn't really need me anymore.

CHAD: Then there are the great painters, of course. Van Gogh was incapable of friendship without self-mutilation and Michelangelo shunned intimate contact ... [*considering*] although his poetry was a little gay.

JASPER: She doesn't look at me the way she used to.

CHAD: Musicians are the most tortured artists of all. Beethoven had his heart broken a thousand times!

He turns and snaps his fingers at SASHA, *finding the appropriate idol to use against her.*

ACT TWO

And Cobain! Look no further than Cobain! That man suffered for something beautiful.

> SASHA *lights up. She has been completely taken in.* CHAD *smiles at her and then turns his gaze back, sharply, catching* JASPER *before he can return to* THEO.

When you come to terms with your true self, as they all did, you will commit your soul to creative pursuits. You will be worthy.

> *He looks disdainfully down at* THEO.

You will be free.

> THEO *looks up, her cheeks tear-stained. She stares out into the distance.*
>
> *Behind her, the dinner setting disappears completely into the red haze that has been gradually rising throughout* CHAD*'s toxic sermon.*
>
> *White strobes flicker.*

THEO: [*whispering*] Anni … Anni …

> *She grabs her stomach. Something is wrong with the baby.*

SCENE ELEVEN

THEO *picks herself up from the floor.*

THEO: [*calling*] Anni!

> ANNI *appears. Behind her, the faces of the famous historical artists, luminaries and entertainers blink on and off one at a time. With each blink they grow more fractured, even desiccated, as visions of madness, addiction and neglect replace the glossy headshots with their bright eyes and flawless smiles.*

ANNI: So you're looking for me now? Way to be consistent, Theo.

> *Once again, the two are identically dressed.* THEO *raises her hand.* ANNI *mirrors the action.* THEO *twirls,* ANNI *does the same, keeping perfect time. All of this unnerves* THEO.

[*With a giggle*] Monkey see, monkey do.

> THEO *shakes her head to clear it.* ANNI *copies.*

Is this a game?

She wilts, disappointed, as THEO *turns away from her.*

THEO: Wallace still wants to get married.
ANNI: [*shrugging*] Marry him.
THEO: I'm not sure it will work.
ANNI: [*shrugging*] Don't marry him. What do I care?

THEO *eyes* ANNI *shrewdly.*

THEO: You've been crying too.

Suddenly self-conscious, ANNI *wipes her cheeks.*

ANNI: I've been *listening*, Theo. Who else do you think you've been whingeing to all this time? Sharing your issues, your angst …

She weaves between the frozen dinner ensemble.

'Daddy doesn't care' … wah … 'Nobody puts *me* first' … wah … 'Why can't I just be anonymous for fifteen minutes?!' … wah, wah, wah!

Again, white strobes flicker. THEO *clutches her belly until they pass. A baby's cry echoes faintly, picking up from* ANNI'*s sarcastic wails.*

And I've been trying to help. That's the pitiful thing! I've been desperate for your approval. I know you're not happy … I know, believe me, that there's something inside you … waiting to burst out!

She reaches for THEO'*s belly and the strobes go haywire.* THEO *shrinks away. The lights take a while to pass, leaving* THEO *breathless.*

I'm your captive audience, Theodora Sprout.

The penny drops …

THEO *looks down at her belly and then snaps back up to stare at the figure in front of her.*

THEO: [*gasping*] I didn't … how could I know?
ANNI: I've been waiting for you to surprise me—*inspire* me—but it's not going to go that way for us, is it? You've already decided to curl up and rot. This is the part where you let it all slip away: the grand finale to your tragic non-drama.

THEO: I didn't see you. You were right there and I didn't … [*Her eyes widen.*] Jesus, I'm just like …

> *Her eyes turn to take in* JASPER, *still frozen.*

ANNI: [*pointedly*] Just like.

> *Beat.*

THEO: [*swallowing*] I've disappointed you.

> *Beat.*

You think my life is 'pedestrian.'

ANNI: [*shouting*] I think you're ordinary, which is precisely what you wanted!

> THEO *feels it as a physical blow from deep inside her belly.*

THEO: And I think that terrifies you, Anni. Because what if that's all there has *ever* been … ordinary people doing their best. Just hanging out together, touching each other's lives, spinning around the sun …

> *It takes all of* THEO*'s strength to approach* ANNI. *She winces as she walks, as though something is still kicking furiously inside of her.*

What if beauty really is in the eye of the beholder and the present is where life is *supposed* to be lived?

> ANNI *takes a step back, judging* THEO.

ANNI: You've never even had the courage to find out. I wanted you to be brilliant!

THEO: I know.

ANNI: [*pleading*] Why won't you even try?

THEO: Because.

ANNI: Because …?

> THEO *sighs.*

THEO: What if art is humble?

> *Beat.*

Dad thinks it's about soaring higher than everybody else, and leaving the deepest mark, but he's forgotten how he started. He's forgotten who he was. It's about the lives we touch while we're here.

ANNI: You're settling.

THEO: I'm not settling, I'm *choosing*.

> ANNI *takes another step back.*

We don't all need to be remembered. I'm going to be temporary and I'm going to be kind. [*Gently*] I'm going to be a mother. Isn't that enough for you, Anni?

ANNI: All children are disappointed by their parents.

> *This stings* THEO.

No ...

> *Beat.*

No, that's not everything ...

> *She summons her courage.*

I don't want to hold you back.

> *Beat.*

THEO: You won't. You haven't. I get it even if you don't, Anni. [*Smiling*] *You* are my work of art.

> *Beat.*
>
> ANNI *raises an eyebrow.*

ANNI: Well, that's ... entirely pathetic.

THEO: [*downcast*] I thought we were about to bond.

ANNI: [*ignoring her*] And it's not even honest! I was a mistake!

THEO: Well ...

ANNI: I was a bad TV night, two shots of tequila and about fifteen seconds of—

THEO: Anni!

ANNI: Look, I love you, Mum ... but I can't be your everything. [*Sincerely*] I need more!

> THEO *grabs her stomach and cries out. It's a mutiny in there.*

Fight with me.

THEO: That's ... not very mature.

ANNI: Fuck mature! Fight! Show me what Grandpa doesn't see!

THEO: I don't want to hurt—

ANNI: *Fight!*

THEO: [*exploding*] Your hemline is disgraceful!

ACT TWO

ANNI: Brilliant!

THEO: You look brassy ... and you know what else? You're pretentious! Strutting around like you're Brigitte Bardot.

She winces. The baby is still kicking up a storm, but THEO *isn't backing down.*

All you need is some skanky tights and a bowler hat, and one of those long cigarette holders for people who don't know how to smoke properly. Maybe a feather boa. What the hell are they even for? It's not a snake, it's not a bird, so what the fuck is it?

ANNI *opens her mouth.*

I haven't finished! You're going to go to work, young lady. If you think I'm turning into an ATM for a demented bohemian you've got another thing coming! You're going to save, you're going to invest prudently, you're going to plan for your future and I'm going to be there, embarrassing you, every step of the way! And do you wanna know why? Because I'm the Queen of Numbers!

Finally, she stands up straight, speaking through the pain.

It's not just two plus two equals four. Not just multiply these digits, subtract that one, find the per centage, predict the loss, calculate the expenses, use that accrual system.

ANNI: [*blinking*] What accrual system?

THEO: Hush! [*Building*] I can balance gorgeous columns of numbers. Cash flows and shareholders' equity elegantly proved, accounts receivable and payable exquisitely calculated. Numbers are my song. I feel the form of an algorithm, I see the symmetry, I get the whole qualitative unity thing ... I'm wired for it.

ANNI: Mum, you're scaring me.

THEO: Give me numbers ... I'll sense the rhythm in the patterns and picture how they fit together, so that they're *glorious!*

She spreads her arms. Numbers fly every which way, arranging themselves.

It's poetry! The wonder of the imaginary number, the intrigue of zero—Bertrand Russell knew—mathematics is both truth and supreme beauty. Maths is my conscious and my unconscious, it's how I create, it's what I breathe! And I don't care if it makes me—

ANNI: It doesn't.

> ANNI *walks over to her, intrigued.*

There you are, Theodora Sprout. So ordinary, so extraordinary.

> THEO *beckons to her daughter with one hand. She is still unsure, yet growing in confidence.*

THEO: But none of this means anything to you.
ANNI: That was never the point.

> *Between them, the flickering strobes become a single white light that swells in intensity until it is impossible to look at.*
>
> *Finally, the light flares and dies ...* THEO *stands alone.*

SCENE TWELVE

The red haze vanishes as the dinner party bursts back into action. JASPER *is hyped.*

JASPER: It's about time I fulfilled my needs. I've been neglecting them ever since …

> *His eyes drift back to* THEO, *who is absently stroking her belly.*
>
> *Beat.*

[*To* CHAD] What would I have to do?
CHAD: To be extraordinary, you must have extraordinary values.
JASPER: [*nodding*] It's like you say in your tapes: 'Self-actualisation isn't selfish …'
JASPER / CHAD: [*together*] '… it's just thorough'.

> WALLACE *has moved to* THEO*'s side.*

WALLACE: You're both drunk on your own conceit.
CHAD: [*to* JASPER] There's still time, my friend. Monet had to wait until his wife *died* before he started painting! [*Dismissive*] No offense.

> BABS *says nothing, her eyes on the table.* CHAD *circles* JASPER.

You'll need a new look, of course. We'll have to pierce something.

> SASHA *joins them.*

SASHA: A horseshoe. You could totally rock a horseshoe! Or venom bites! [*Pointing to her tongue*] Right here!

ACT TWO

CHAD: Think of it as a cleansing. Not just a physical, but a *spiritual* transformation.

SASHA: You're a sexy butterfly bursting free!

CHAD: Ooh, I like that! Bursting free of domesticity, leaving poor choice and obligation behind.

WALLACE: How can one carcass hold so much hot air? Are you really suggesting that art should be more important than people?

CHAD: [*laughing*] Oh, my sweet, simple Wally ... art *is* more important than people.

WALLACE: Sasha, this guy is the opposite of everything we stand for.

SASHA: Like you stand for anything. You chose to be ordinary, so go build a house in the suburbs, buy yourself a Labradoodle. Some of us want more.

WALLACE: And yet you're chasing so much less.

> SASHA *raises her lollipop and moves in for the kill.* CHAD *stops her, gently.*

CHAD: [*to* WALLACE] Here's a lesson in politics, boy. During the Second World War, Churchill sent valuable artworks to Canada. He knew people would die ... frankly, he expected it ... but people can be replaced. Look at the tribal paintings we covet from the very cultures we discard, the songs we revere that tell stories of slavery and injustice ... the same stories that we skip by on the nightly news.

WALLACE: It's not that simple, Chad.

CHAD: But it *is* that simple, and we *like* it that way. We like objects. We like pretty colours and catchy tunes.

> *He looms over* WALLACE.

How many real people can you honestly say you give a fuck about?

WALLACE: More than you'd think.

> WALLACE *kisses* THEO's *forehead.*

CHAD: Pfft. So young. [*To* JASPER] Art separates the cultured from the barbaric. This is what you have to offer.

JASPER: I can be that special?

CHAD: [*softening*] Don't you see? This is what distinguishes you from the walking dead out there ... from the blue-collar masses with their babies, their mortgages and their petty little problems.

He closes in on JASPER.

Seven billion people on this rock and only a handful—a precious few—are capable of being heard. Take the opportunities I can offer you and you will be more than a husband or a father, you will be remembered and cherished, and—

FIGSBY: What's the point?

Beat.

All eyes land on FIGSBY.

CHAD: What's the point? [*Scoffing*] Seriously?

Beat.

FIGSBY *nods.*

FIGSBY: What's the point?

CHAD *is speechless.*

Explain it to me.

She waits.

CHAD: Jasper has a gift.

FIGSBY: Don't give us that superior crap. If he leaves all of this behind … [*gesturing*] if he forgets his family and his home, and everything that's real—

CHAD: He won't forget. [*To* JASPER] You will rise above.

FIGSBY: If he becomes a cruel, selfish, empty person then what is the fucking point?

CHAD: Well, I … [*He clears his throat.*] Art transcends!

FIGSBY: What does that even mean?

CHAD: Its value is immeasurable! It underpins society, it provokes debate, it … it just … it … it's really important, okay?

FIGSBY *looks directly at* JASPER.

FIGSBY: Those seven billion people he talks about … most of them are lonely, most of them are starving.

SASHA: [*embarrassed*] Figsby—

FIGSBY: No, I need to say this. [*To* JASPER] Those people would fight for what you have. They wouldn't give it all away.

CHAD: Everyone's a critic, Jasper.

FIGSBY: Shut your stupid face!

She sighs.

Would you really leave them …

She points to THEO *and her unborn child.* THEO *stares back.*

… to be with your ego?

JASPER *slowly puts his glass down. He locks eyes with* BABS, *shakes his head and reaches for his coat.*

CHAD *shoots a smug smile straight at* FIGSBY, *who throws her arms up in disgust.*

THEO: Dad.

JASPER *stops.*

Mathematically, it's a fizzer, but … [*Resigned*] You do what you have to do.

He looks back at THEO, *unsure.*

JASPER: And do you think I can?
THEO: Of course. You can do anything.

She wipes away a fresh tear.

You're my dad.

JASPER *takes this in. Hesitates. Perhaps it was all he needed.*
Beat.
He carries his coat over to THEO *and lays it over her shoulders.*
THEO *cries in her father's arms. He cradles her for a long time before he speaks.*

JASPER: It's okay. I'm here.

He wipes her eyes.

I'm a fogey, and a fool … but I'm here.

THEO *takes a while to recover and form words of her own.*

THEO: I never meant to hold you back.
JASPER: Sssh. Don't be crazy. [*Swallowing*] You're my favourite person, Theo. [*Smiling faintly*] You're the person I invented.

She laughs through her tears.

THEO: My friends don't think you're 'hip'.

JASPER: I don't think anyone does.

He pulls her into a hug and holds her there, speaking softly.

I've been chasing the dream for so long. At some point, I let it get scary.

Beat.

Time to wake up.

He is speaking half to himself and half to his daughter. Slowly, they share a smile and stand together.

CHAD *watches them carefully. He knows the tide has turned against him.*

CHAD: Jasper, I'm only calling it as I see it. To be a success, you have to make hard choices. To be extraordinary, you have to—and I know it's rough—let the ordinary fall by the wayside.

JASPER ignores him. He has one arm over THEO, *and places the other over* BABS. *They stare* CHAD *down together, as a family.*

You don't want to wake up in another twenty years full of regret, do you? Because I've seen that! I've seen—

He swallows.

I've *been* that. [*Raw*] Jasper, I've been you. Now all I want is to save you from an ordinary life. These people are dragging you down into the mediocre!

JASPER: No, they're not. That's just the excuse I made for myself. [*Looking around*] I'm at my best when I'm with these people.

CHAD: Your best? Well, I guess you're not so special after all.

THEO: And I guess you must be very lonely.

CHAD *scowls at her.* BABS *steps in his way.*

BABS: Chad dear, I'm afraid I want you out of my house. I expect you mean well, but … the thing is … you're killing the vibe.

He opens his mouth to reply, only to have FIGSBY *shove his cape right in his face.*

FIGSBY: Don't forget your chamanto!

Suddenly small, wounded, CHAD *fidgets with the garment in his hand. He turns to leave. Stops. Turns back.*

CHAD: Does anyone have any spare change for the bus?

    JASPER *reaches into his pocket, pays* CHAD *and gestures to the door. Everyone exhales.*

JASPER: I've been such a douche.

BABS: Yes, but you're the douche I married.

    She kisses his cheek.

Don't get me wrong, pet ... you *will* make this up to us. You're coming to the fête on Sunday, and you're wearing gingham.

WALLACE: What about you, Sash? No hard feelings?

SASHA: …

WALLACE: Right. There are lots of hard feelings. Hard, durable, heavy-duty feelings.

SASHA: You stood up to him.

WALLACE: A bit.

SASHA: You stood up to me.

WALLACE: [*mortified*] Shit. Sorry. Truly sorry.

SASHA: Don't apologise, mingeface. [*Smiling*] You might make a politician yet.

WALLACE: [*brightening*] Really?

SASHA: Really.

WALLACE: Well, okay then! Nice work, people!

    He points to the door, where CHAD *has recently exited.*

Good riddance, eh? What a cock-knocker!

    WALLACE *turns to see* JASPER, *staring him down.*

JASPER: You made me a granddad.

    Beat.

WALLACE: Theo helped.

JASPER: I'm too sexy to be a granddad.

WALLACE: [*terrified*] Yes. Yes, sir. Yes, you are.

JASPER: I have nice skin.

WALLACE: Yes, you do.

    Beat.

JASPER *maintains his stern tone.*

JASPER: Should we expect wedding bells?
THEO: Not today.

She untangles herself from her father, smiling playfully.

Stop giving my boyfriend the third degree, Gramps.
JASPER: [*grinning*] Hey!
THEO: Papa.
JASPER: Theo!
THEO: Paddle Pop.
BABS: Gammy.
THEO: Wrinkle cheeks.
BABS: Poop drawers.
JASPER: Give me a break.

He's still smiling.

THEO: You don't think you're getting off easily, do you? After letting that roach through our door?
JASPER: I wanted to sing.
THEO: So sing! Get the band back together, book a week in the studio, invite Shred Lord over for tea and bucket bongs ... but have fun for Buddha's sake! Don't turn it into an obsession! [*In a little voice*] I love you, you fuckwit.
JASPER: Yeah?
THEO: I don't always like you, but ...
WALLACE: He can sing when we tie the knot.

THEO *approaches* WALLACE.

THEO: Save that ring for another rainy day. We have to try living together for a while first.
WALLACE: Theo, are you *still* trying to move in with me?
THEO: Come on ... seriously, you can't leave us alone with these two.
WALLACE: Us?
THEO: [*nodding*] Us.

She puts his hand on her belly.

She's going to be trouble. Those Jasper genes are pretty robust.
WALLACE: I'm not sure I can promise you an ordinary life.

THEO: [*shrugging*] We'll give it our best shot.

She puts her arms around him.

FIGSBY: Psst. Kiss her. Show her the moves, like we practised.

WALLACE looks back at FIGSBY, annoyed. THEO gently places a finger under his chin and steers his gaze until he is looking directly into her eyes.

THEO: I'll show you.

A guitar riff starts up.

She kisses him.

Red beams crisscross the stage.

Once again, the riff is unmistakable ... 'Sweet Child of Mine' (Guns 'N' Roses).

JASPER belts out the song. One by one the other lights fade until only the red rock fantasy remains.

The mirror ball casts flashes of silver, smoke rises and the rest of the cast become dancing shadows, but JASPER keeps his eyes locked on his daughter—his favourite person.

THEO and JASPER are the last to vanish, together.

THE END

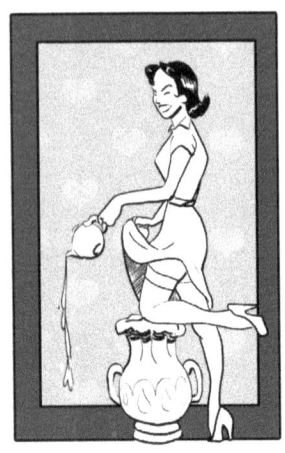  

Barbara Sprout   Jasper Sprout   Chad Mombardo

Wallace Bobbottom   Sasha Flint   Imani Fisseha Azikiwe

www.ingramcontent.com/pod-product-compliance
Lightning Source LLC
Chambersburg PA
CBHW050016090426
42734CB00021B/3292